FATE & THE TWILIGHT OF THE GODS

THE NORNS AND AN EXEGESIS OF VÖLUSPÁ

GWENDOLYN TAUNTON

MANTICORE PRESS

FATE & THE TWILIGHT OF THE GODS:
THE NORNS & AN EXEGESIS OF VÖLUSPÁ
Gwendolyn Taunton

© Manticore Press (Australia, 2018)

All rights reserved, no section of this book may be utilized without permission, including electronic reproductions without the permission of the author and publisher. Published in Australia.

Thema Classification: QRSW (Norse Religion), DBSN (Icelandic & Norse Literature), VXWS (Paganism)

978-0-6482996-6-0

MANTICORE PRESS
WWW.MANTICORE.PRESS

CONTENTS

THE NORNIR AND THE CONCEPT OF FATE 7

THE TWILIGHT OF THE GODS: AN EXEGESIS OF VÖLUSPÁ 59

This book is dedicated to Loki for providing me with firsthand experience of Ragnarök in the form of 10,000 plus earthquakes.

PART I

THE NORNIR & THE CONCEPT OF FATE

I want to learn more and more to see as beautiful what is necessary in things; then I shall be one of those who make things beautiful. *Amor fati*: let that be my love henceforth!
- *Friedrich Nietzsche*

FATE IS BY DEFINITION A FORCE THAT remains beyond the realm of normal human control, consisting of circumstances that are unavoidable and small actions which often result in disproportional consequences—these are the acts of the mysterious hand of destiny—which can only be described as supernatural or divine intervention. Even the very act of attempting to avoid a fated outcome can be sufficient to create the necessary environment that will result in it being caused to occur. Fate, therefore, can only be a form of predestination and its effect—for good or ill—is unavoidable for both Gods and mortals alike.

In the Traditions of Northern Europe, fate is usually represented as a Tripartite Goddess consisting of three aspects, known collectively as the Norns or Nornir. Although reference is frequently made to the Nornir, they remain as shadowy figures, controlling the fate of the cosmos from deep within the shadows beneath Yggdrasill, the *axis mundi* of Norse mythology. Rather than being individual deities, the Nornir seem to form their own unique trinity which remains distinct from both the Æsir and the Vanir, but they are nonetheless able to control mortals. The conspicuous ambiguity of the Nornir presents three possibilities for their lack of personification:

- The Nornir were imported from a non-indigenous Tradition which gradually merged with that of the existing Tradition via the Roman military incursions into Europe and trade agreements with Scandinavia.

- The Nornir are an anthropomorphism of a philosophical idea explaining the interaction of time and human activity within the perspective of a recognized cosmic order which is indicative of a belief in predestination.

- The Nornir are part of an older Tradition with possible connections to the Proto-Indo-European substratum.

To identify the primary role of the Nornir and the nature of their interactions with both humans and Gods, the most logical place to start is with their surviving textual references.

When researching the myths and traditions of Europe, there is an additional layer of complexity because important aspects of the Tradition no longer exist, due to the widespread destruction of literature by Christians during their aggressive conversion of Europeans. Therefore, any writer on the topic has to face the prospect that what they are currently examining could well have been part of a larger corpus of material prior to the advent of Christianity in Europe. What may at first appear to be a very simplistic idea could have originally been more complex, and only the basic outline of this ideology has persisted into the modern era. In this regard, the Nornir may well be a lot more than a Tripartite Goddess, and could conceal a more intricate philosophical and/or metaphysical structure which has been erased from the history books.

IMAGES OF FATE: DEPICTIONS OF THE NORNIR

> I have heard that up north in an island,
> [the/a] Norn is grim to me,
> Oðinn chose him much too soon,
> Þórólfr has met his end;
> The heaviness of old age
> - *Egils Saga*[1]

The Nornir are usually represented as a Tripartite entity. This depiction is supported by *Fáfnismál*,

---

[1] BEK-PEDERSON, J., *The Norns in Old Norse Mythology* (Scotland: Dunedin Academic Press Ltd, 2011), 15

which, in turn, may be drawing on conceptions similar to those underlying the First Merseburg Charm.[2] Not only are the Nornir split into three distinct entities, what is also of importance is that the three Nornir have names – and each play a different role in the construction of an individual's fate. Respectively, the most common names for the Nornir are Urðr, Verðandi, and Skuld. They are associated with the temporal states of past, present, and future, as is seen in the following extract.

> Thence wise-maidens three betake them –
> Under spreading boughs their bower stands –
> Urðr one is hight, the other, Verðandi,
> Skuld the third: they scores did cut,
> They laws did make, they lives did choose:
> For the children of men they marked their fates.[3]

These Nornir are the most widely known portrayals, however, references concerning the nature of the Nornir and their number sometimes varies. Furthermore, the names for the Nornir are sometimes found outside of explicit references to them, which is suggestive of the Nornir possessing additional functions or a more esoteric significance which is not fully conveyed by surviving textual

---

[2] BEK-PEDERSON, J., *The Norns in Old Norse Mythology*, 41
[3] WINTERBOURNE, A., *When the Norns have Spoken: Time and Fate in Germanic Paganism* (USA: Associated University Press, 2004), 57

references. For example, Urðr (genitive *urðar*, plural *urðir*), appears in fifteen or sixteen instances, either as the name of a Norn or in compounds where it has the meaning of 'fate' or 'fateful'; Skuld occurs in four instances outside of the *Völuspá* and *Snorra-Edda*: as a noun or perhaps simply as abstract 'fate' in *Grógaldr*, as a Valkyrjur in *Þulur*, as a Heiti for a woman in *Lausavísa*, and as the evil half-sister of Hrólfr in *Hrólfs Saga*.[4] Of the three Nornir, it is Skuld who appears to have the greatest degree of both complexity and personification, which also indicates that she is either the most powerful or the most feared member of the trinity. The variation in terminology likewise provides an indication that the Nornir are not just an anthropomorphism of a chronological concept. Accordingly, the rudimentary temporal aspect of the Norns is likely to be the lesser function which is part of a more complex whole.

There are other collectives of semi-divine female figures to be found in Scandinavian and Teutonic mythology which possess some similarities to the Norns—namely the Dísir, Fylgjur, and Valkyrjur—all three of which also have a link to the destinies of mortals. Whilst not explicitly tied to fate, these entities are allotted a protective role which enables them to guide the destinies of their respective wards, and as such, need to be examined in relation to the Nornir. The Dísir, in particular, have previously been looked at in connection to the Nornir, though

---

[4] BEK-PEDERSON, J., *The Norns in Old Norse Mythology*, 76

the exact identity of the Dísir themselves also appears to be a topic of contention. For example, Gunnell states that unlike the other type of beings (Fylgjur and Valkyrjur), the Dísir sometimes receive sacrifices, have places dedicated to them, and appear to protect not only individuals but also families, and even nations.[5] Raudvere, by contrast, claims the following:

> The function of the Dísir seems to have been the protection of crops and production in a certain place. They are more closely related to the landscape and have a more markedly protective role than the abstract Fylgjur. The latter are connected to an individual or family, while the Dísir seem primarily connected to a certain place.[6]

Whatever aspect the Dísir play, whether it be protecting families of the land or the land itself, it is obvious that the Dísir are ancestral guardian spirits. However, they do still have supernatural abilities above and beyond the norm of a mere specter. Further clarification on the role of the Dísir is provided by De Vries and Prokorny, who both cite etymological evidence that the word Dísir derives from the Vedic language, with De Vries linking the Dísir to *dhiṣaṇyant* (attentive, devout) and Prokorny then linking dhiṣaṇyant to the Sanskrit

---

[5] BEK-PEDERSON, J., *The Norns in Old Norse Mythology*, 42
[6] Ibid.

root *dhī* (to see) from which the Sanskrit word for wisdom, thought, and insight derives.[7] What is also particularly telling about this terminology is that the Sanskrit root is often used in descriptive passages about the ṛṣi, the seers who composed the *Rig Veda*. Thus, the implication is not that the word describes the normal mode of eyesight, but rather a preternatural form of vision that enables them to see through the veils of *maya* and see the world as it really is. From these terms connected to the Dísir, it seems clear that they (albeit still possessing a minor influence over the course of human fate) are not the same as the Nornir—rather they are a form of ancestral guardian which possesses precognitive vision in the same manner as the Vedic seers remembering, of course, that the Vedic seers are themselves the ancestors of the traditional Brahmin caste.

Though sometimes compared to the Dísir and the Nornir, the Valkyrjur appear to be something different again. The Valkryjur tend to manifest in heroic poetry and are often portrayed as the daughters of kings who, for reasons mostly unexplained, are leading a masculine lifestyle. Descriptions of the Valkryjur show them as young, unmarried women who, for some reason, have become warriors and take on an entirely masculine demeanor, only to undergo dramatic changes back into a feminine role when they encounter the hero

---

[7] BEK-PEDERSON, J., *The Norns in Old Norse Mythology*, 42

and become betrothed or married to him.⁸ However, they are additionally referred to as a battleground spirit which Oðinn sends forth to collect the souls of heroes that have fallen in combat and conduct them to Valhalla, or protect mortal men, as Grimm says here: "wish-maidens fetch his wish-sons [...] But these messengers also take charge of heroes while alive, and protect them until death: they are guardian-angels and death-angels."⁹ Thus, there seems to be a confusion of terminology between mortal women and a guardian spirit in textual references, perhaps with the name being applied in an allegorical sense for mortal women.[10]

Of the other groups of supernatural female figures in the Northern Traditions, the remaining two which could possibly have a link to the Nornir are the Fylgjur and the Volur. Of these two types, the Fylgjur do not appear to make decisions or choices concerning fate or destiny and probably operate as a form of 'luck spirit' for the person to whom they are attached.[11] Similarly, the Volur, though having knowledge of the destinies of mortals, are represented as human women, not supernatural

---

[8] BEK-PEDERSON, J., *The Norns in Old Norse Mythology*, 55

[9] GRIMM, J., *Teutonic Mythology Volume II* (USA: Dover Publications, 2004), 840

[10] A role similar to the Yogini/Dakini or Daimon, but linked more strongly to warfare. However, the Yogini/Dakini can adopt a similar function in Tantrism, as a form of 'Daimon/Anima' hybrid.

[11] BEK-PEDERSON, J., *The Norns in Old Norse Mythology*, 60

ones. It is also apparent that although the Volur may have foreknowledge of certain events, they neither allot nor allocate specific events to individuals. The knowledge possessed by the Volur is more akin to that of the sage or shamanic stream than it is of a divine origin.

On the basis of these comparisons, it seems apparent that any link between the Nornir, Dísir, Valkryjur, Flygjur, and the Volur is tenuous at best and that these groups of female figures do not overlap in any regard, except that the said mythological groupings all contain female entities. The fact that the name Skuld appears as the name of both a Norn and a Valkryjur appears to be coincidental. The only common factor between them is the form of literary content they appear in. The Nornir, Dísir, and Valkyrjur hardly ever turn up in mythological poems; with the exception of *Völuspá*, they are mentioned almost exclusively in heroic and skaldic poetry.[12] However, this does not indicate that there is any degree of relation between the three groups which would prove that the entities are the same. Rather the Nornir, the Dísir, and the Valkyrjur all tend to appear in the heroic and skaldic poetry because they interact and impact on mortals more than they do the Gods. The Dísir and the Valkyrjur protect mortals, whilst the Nornir have the power to write their fate.

---

[12] BEK-PEDERSON, J., *The Norns in Old Norse Mythology*, 41

Though the Nornir are usually referred to as a collective group, there are also references to isolated or lone Nornir. Snorri Sturluson makes a direct reference to the multiplicity of the Nornir in the following passage.

> These maidens shape men's lives. We call them Norns. There are also other Norns who visit everyone when they are born to shape their lives…Good Norns, ones of noble parentage, shape good lives, but as for those people that become the victims of misfortune, it is evil Norns that are responsible.[13]

This may be a confusion on Snorri's part, however, as he may well be erroneously associating the Dísir and Flygjur with Nornir here. In the majority of references, the Nornir are portrayed as a trinity, consisting of Urðr, Verðandi, and Skuld, who are morally ambivalent as opposed to 'good' or 'evil'.

Outside of literature, evidence for the existence of the Nornir is scant – which is not particularly surprising since a lot of content may well have been destroyed, either by the advent of Christianity in Europe, or as result of the ravages of time itself. However, the items which have survived strongly support the premise that there are only three Nornir. By way of example, there are three female figures depicted on the right panel of Franks

---

[13] BEK-PEDERSON, J., *The Norns in Old Norse Mythology*, 76

Casket, an Anglo-Saxon whalebone chest from the eighth century, which has been identified as a representation of the Nornir. In addition to this, the inscription N 351 M from the stave church at Borgund says,

> Þórir carved these runes on the eve of Olausmass when he traveled past here. The Norns did both good and evil, great toil [...] they created for me.

Finally, there is an inscribed wooden stick from Søndre Engelgården at Bryggen in Bergen, which specifically uses the word Nornir.[14] Other than these artifacts, the strongest evidence for three Nornir are the Roman-inspired votive altars depicting three 'mothers'. The existence of these altars also provides proof of a direct connection between the Nornir and the Roman Parcae, another trinity of female figures, almost identical to the Nornir.

THE ORIGIN OF THE NORNS

In Roman mythology, the Parcae were the offspring of Nox (Night) and Erebus (Hell).[15] The Parcae themselves are a derivative of the Moirai from

---

[14] BEK-PEDERSON, J., *The Norns in Old Norse Mythology*, 9
[15] WINTERBOURNE, A., *When the Norns have Spoken: Time and Fate in Germanic Paganism*, 84

Hellenic Tradition, in which the Moirai are also referred to as the daughters of Nyx (the Greek name for Nox). This is described by Hesiod, although he also states that these three Goddesses were the daughters of Zeus and the Goddess Themis. According to later Orphic Tradition, the Moirai resided in the heavens, in a cave by the pool where white water flows.[16] The Moirai are named Klotho (The Spinner), Lachesis (The Apportioner), and Atropos (The Inevitable). Homer, however, speaks of a single Moira, a spinning Goddess who is 'strong', 'hard to endure', and 'destroying',[17] which is most likely a composite entity composed of the three Moirai.

The Ancient Greek word *moira* (μοίρα) means a portion or lot of the whole, and is related to *meros* (part, lot) and *moros* (fate, doom). It is also related to the Latin *meritum* (desert, reward) and the English word merit, which is derived from the Indo-European root *(s)mer* meaning 'to allot, assign'. Given that the name Moirai stems from the word moira, which means portion or number, the Orphists claimed that the Moirai corresponded to that of the three phases of the moon; and that is why Orpheus sings of "the Moirai in white raiment".[18] The association with the moon may not, however,

---

[16] Compare with the dwelling place of the Nornir by the well under Yggdrasil.

[17] KERÉNYI, C., *The Gods of the Greeks* (UK: Thames and Hudson, 1961), 32

[18] Ibid.

be correct—the part or portion may simply refer to aspects of life for each soul which is created by the spinning of the Fates, in a similar aspect to 'past, becoming, and future'—which is a predominant characteristic of the Nornir.

> The part or length of the yarn that they assign to each mortal is decided solely by them and not even Zeus can influence their decision. Even Zeus and the other Greek Gods are deemed to be powerless against the will of the Moirai. The most that Zeus can do is to take his golden scales, preferably at noon, and measure—in the case, for example, of two opponents—which of them is doomed to die that day.[19]

As was seen previously with the Nornir, there appears to have been a certain amount of fluctuation in regards to the number of Moirai. Although they were usually depicted as a trinity, there are some variations to this rule. For example, in a famous vase-painting depicting the marriage of the Goddess Thetis with the mortal Peleus they are depicted as four in number and at Delphi only two of them are worshiped:[20] a Moira of Birth and a Moira of Death.[21]

---

[19] KERÉNYI, C., *The Gods of the Greeks*, 32

[20] The duality at Delphi is connected to the dyad between Apollo and Dionysus, overlaid on top of an earlier Goddess based Tradition.

[21] KERÉNYI, C., *The Gods of the Greeks*, 32

There are other groups of female figures with similarity to the Moirai, just as there are with the Nornir. Like the Moirai, the Graiai are described as 'Grey Goddesses'. Of the Graiai however, Hesiod relates only the names of two: Pemphredo, of the beautiful raiment, and Enyo, of the saffron raiment.[22] The third group of Grey Goddesses in Hellenic mythology is the Erinyes (also known as the Maniai or Furies). They are described as being older than Zeus with black skin and rainment of grey[23] and are either children of Gaia[24] or are the daughters of Nyx.[25]

Outside of Greece and Rome, there are further instances of Tripartite Goddesses presiding over fate. Other examples can be found in the legends of the Saamis which portray a similar trinity composed of Sarakka, Juksakka, and Uksakka, along with the three daughters of Conaran in the Celtic Tradition.

As to the question of why the Fates are so dominant in a broad spectrum of Traditions on the European continent, two solutions present themselves. The first hypothesis is that the original

---

[22] KERÉNYI, C., *The Gods of the Greeks*, 45

[23] Ibid., 46

[24] In her chthonic role as the 'Black Earth Mother', Gaia also presides over dreams and the underworld, in similar manner to Hades – this is why Persephone is the wife of Hades. In this aspect Gaia rules the world underground (Hades) as well as the fertile soil above the surface, and in this aspect Gaia gives birth to the Furies, hence their dark skin and connections with punishment.

[25] KERÉNYI, C., *The Gods of the Greeks*, 47

basis of the Nornir were the Greek Moirai, and that their worship was dispersed through the European continent by the Romans (who absorbed much of the Hellenic Tradition into their own) during their incursions into Europe and via trade routes into Scandinavia. There is no evidence of the Nornir prior to the arrival of the Romans.

It is also feasible that the belief in the Fates is a remnant of a Indo-European Tradition. However, if this were the case we could expect to see a similar Tripartite Goddess in India,[26] and evidence of this absent. It is possible that the Fates (including the Moirai, Parcae, Nornir, and all their equivalents) could, in fact, be an anthropomorphism of an abstract cosmological principle inherited from the Indo-Europeans, which became progressively conceptualized and less abstract. Before reaching a decision on the origins of the Nornir though, there is one more theory which requires examination: that they are connected to the three maidens from Jötunheimr.

In *Völuspá* there is a reference to a Golden Age which persisted until three giant maidens emerged from Jötunheimr. It is implied within *Völuspá* that the end of the Golden Age is explicitly connected with the arrival of these women from Jötunheimr. Using this specific part of *Völuspá* as a reference point, S. N. Hagen attempts to substantiate an

---

[26] Unless there is reason to associate the trinity formed by Pārvatī, Durga, and Kālī to this, but initially this seems highly unlikely.

etymological correspondence between 'North' and 'Nornir', offering the following as evidence:

> ON. Nornir is probably a substantivized adjective like Heinir, the only difference between them being one of *gelnder*; cf. *gestir*, m., *urbiir*, f. Its immediate phonetic predecessor must have been **no (r) nir*, 'beings from the north.'[27]

In support of this claim, Hagen also cites both Hel and Jötunheimr as being located in the North, saying that Jötunheimr is described as being located in the north, or in the east, which he states as being in the direction of the White Sea.[28] This would place the Nornir as having an entry point into the Northern Traditions coming from the region of the north of Russia—a location which is at odds with both earlier theories that the Nornir could be a Indo-European feature,[29] and that the Nornir could have been based on the Greek Moirai and spread through Europe via the Romans. Hagen's etymological correlation between 'North' and 'Nornir' should be dismissed on the grounds that

---

[27] HAGEN, S. N., On. Nornir 'Fates' in *Modern Language Notes*, Vol. 39, No. 8 (The Johns Hopkins University Press, 1924), 468

[28] Ibid., 467

[29] Unless one accepts the point of origin for IE peoples to be in the far north—which may validate some ideas of a 'Hyperborean Origin'—though I would dismiss this idea personally.

it is overly simplistic and reductionist. The fact that both groups are composed of three female entities does not imply they are the same, and there are clear distinctions between the two triads. The three 'giant maidens' are connected to the concept of evil and Ragnarök. The Fates remain neutral in their interactions with mortals, and are connected to Norse predeterminism.

THE JUDGMENT OF THE NORNIR

> We have fought well,
> We stand on Goth corpses,
> Weary of sword-edge,
> Like eagles on a branch.
> We have won great renown,
> Whether we die now or yesterday
> A man does not live out the evening
> After the Nornir give their verdict.
> - *Hamðismál*[30]

One striking feature of the Nornir appears to be that their decision is not necessarily random, nor is it totally predetermined – to a certain extent, it would seem that the Nornir also perform a judiciary function for a set of fixed cosmic laws. This feature of

---

[30] BEK-PEDERSON, J., *The Norns in Old Norse Mythology*, 24

the Nornir is known as *norna dómr* – the judgment of the Nornir. There is some leeway for human free will though, for their judgment does not appear to be totally decided in advance. However, once the Nornir do pronounce a verdict it is inescapable, for as it says in the *Íslendinga Saga* "*Urðr mun eigi forðask*" – no one can escape fate.[31] On a similar note, *Fáfnismál* cites an example of how the Nornir operate:

> The judgment of the Nornir
> You will have out at sea
> The way stupid men die;
> You will drown in the water
> If you row in a wind:
> All is dangerous for one who is *fey*.[32]

In the above passage, it is obvious that the Nornir pass judgment on those who violate common sense, for one who would row or take a boat out in adverse weather conditions, is obviously 'tempting fate', so to speak. It is extremely likely that in such an incident the Nornir would also pass a heavy verdict and drown the man who committed this act of folly at sea. In this and other passages, there are strong indications that the Nornir operate as a type of 'cosmic law' in which, should ordinary human law fail or not be complied with, the Nornir intervene

---

[31] BEK-PEDERSON, J., *The Norns in Old Norse Mythology*, 24

[32] Ibid., 23

to rectify events in order for important future events to occur in the wider schema. Also in *Gylfaginning*, Urðarbrunnr (the well beneath Yggdrasill) seems to possess significance in a legal or quasi-legal sense, being both the assembly place and court (*dómstaðr*) of the Gods as well as the abode of the Nornir.[33] Moreover, the names of the three primary Nornir provide a strong clue to their respective functions, just as they do with the Greek Moirai (with whom the functions of the respective Nornir are an exact match).

The names of the three primary Nornir are Urðr, Verðandi, and Skuld. The first of the Nornir, Urðr, is an etymological cognate for the Old English *wyrd*. The verb *verða* (to happen, come to pass, take place) is obviously associated with the name of the second Norn Verðandi. The past plural (third-person) form of verða is also *urðu*, describing those things which 'came about' or 'did happen', and the similarity between urðr (fate) and urðu (happened)[34] is what has given rise to the interpretation of Urðr as 'past'. Urðr was the Old Norse form, wyrd the Old English, *wurt* the Germanic, and *wurd* was the Old Saxon equivalent – none of which mean past in a chronological sense.[35] This illustrates the function and sequential process of the first two Nornir; the

---

[33] BEK-PEDERSON, J., *The Norns in Old Norse Mythology*, 91

[34] Ibid.

[35] WINTERBOURNE, A., *When the Norns have Spoken: Time and Fate in Germanic Paganism*, 12

actions decided in advance and those decided in the past, and actions resulting from this which are currently occurring. It does not, however, represent the past in a chronological sense, but rather a form of metaphysical past that involves an element of predeterminism, in the sense that destiny is pre-ordained by the first Norn in the past, with this element being put into play and 'becoming' under the influence of the second Norn. Evidence for predestination in the Northern Traditions is also provided by the following passages: *"lagt er alt for"* (predestined is all) and *"era með löstom lögð æfi þer"* (Sæm. 175b).[36]

Based on the etymology involving these linguistic roots and different uses of the terms for 'fate', an interpretation of the Nornir as 'past, present, and future' is extraordinarily inadequate. Furthermore, the name of the first Norn cannot be connected with a simple notion of a temporal past, for as her name implies, events are predestined to occur. On the basis of this, a better classification of Urðr is as the Norn who creates an individual's fate – she writes their predestined circumstances, their place in the cosmic order, and the role to which each individual is allocated. The second Norn Verðandi represents the active process, the events, or actions surrounding an individual which become destiny. Urðr is the one who first 'spins' the thread of an individual's life, and Verðandi creates the actions which 'fix' the yarn into its allocated position.

---

[36] GRIMM, J., *Teutonic Mythology Volume II*, 861

Finally, it is the third Norn Skuld who decides when to terminate the thread. It is erroneous, however, to equate Skuld with death, for her true role is much more complex than this. Death itself does not kill, but rather comes to collect the dead – it is Skuld and not Hel who cuts the thread of life. Hel, the Death Goddess, does not destroy; she receives the dead into her house.[37] This negative characteristic of Skuld as the Norn who brings death and final judgment persists through the entire spectrum of literature involving her, and presents Skuld as a figure with whom mortals can interact, unlike the other two Nornir.[38] This suggests that Skuld is the aspect of the Nornir who decides an individuals destiny and that communication with Skuld was performed with the hope that one could sway or postpone her verdict.

The name Skuld is related to the noun *skuld*, meaning 'debt' or 'something owed'; and in the Christian interpretation, it later came to mean 'guilt' as well. It is related to the modal verb *skulu*, which correlates with the English 'shall', and has a range of different meaning, including "shall, must, bidding, need, duty, and obligation".[39] Skuld is also described as being 'the youngest Norn', a statement which seems based on an understanding of her as an event encountered in the future that has not yet transpired and is, therefore, 'younger' than the other

---

[37] GRIMM, J., *Teutonic Mythology Volume II*, 839

[38] BEK-PEDERSON, J., *The Norns in Old Norse Mythology*, 76

[39] Ibid., 78

two Nornir. However, the age ascribed to Skuld does not provide a sufficient reason to associate her with any form of chronological period or concept of future as such. Skuld appears to be the embodiment or outcome of actions committed under the influence of the first two Nornir and is more akin to representing a 'final verdict' or a karmic force rather than just a temporal event.

Fate is not a single concept and is linked to the higher cosmic process of judgment similar to karma, as can be seen from the linguistic evidence. There are multiple words for fate, some of which are not yet fully translated. Old Norse alone has six words that cover the concept of fate: *ørlog, skop, miotuðr, auðna, forlog,* and *urðr*.[40] Of these terms, those most commonly used are ørlog (what has been decided from the beginning, what has been experienced), forlog (fate), and skop (what has been pre-determined).[41] In the three forms of fate specified here, it should be reasonably obvious that there is an etymological connection between ørlog and forlog. The semantic link occurs between the two forms of 'fate' and 'law' (log)—for the element log forms part of two words for 'fate'—ørlog and forlog.[42] Furthermore, not all words for fate are employed in connection with the Nornir.[43] This indicates that

---

[40] BEK-PEDERSON, J., *The Norns in Old Norse Mythology*, 165

[41] Ibid., 171

[42] Ibid., 165

[43] Ibid.

the Nornir represent a connection between fate and the cosmic order, and they represent the divine law in contrast to human law. While humans concern themselves with log on the surface, the Nornir concern themselves with the deeper levels, with ørlog, the warp and weft of the cosmic threads, and the foundations of human existence.[44] Furthermore, according to Grimm, it seems that ørlog played a significant role in deciding the outcome of war (which is not especially surprising considering that the results of battle often rely on a number of forces outside of the participant's direct sphere of influence).

> OS. *Ørlag*, AS. *Ørlæg*, denoting a 'fixing from the first'; but as the most momentous issue of fate was to the heathen that of war, it early deviated into the sense of *bellum*, and in Hel. 132, 3 *urlagi bellum* seems distinct from ørlog, *Ørleg fatum*, but in reality are one. So the OHG. *Urteil, urteili*. AS. *Ordœl*, from being the award of a judge, came to mean that of battle.[45]

Fate, in its complete incarnation, involves death as much as it does the flow of life and one who is doomed to an expedited or inevitable death is said to be fey.[46] Such a person is regarded as bound or

---

[44] BEK-PEDERSON, J., *The Norns in Old Norse Mythology*, 165

[45] GRIMM, J., *Teutonic Mythology Volume II*, 857

[46] Ibid., 856

fettered by the Gods, whom are referred to with terms such as 'bonds' or 'fetters', *viz. bönd, höpt.*[47] Tacitus also relates that the Semnones performed a religious observance which involved reverence for a sacred grove, into which no man could enter "unless he is bound with a cord, by which he acknowledges his own inferiority and the power of the deity."[48] This description of being fettered or bound was not exclusive to the Teutonic Tradition either, for this metaphor was also used by the Romans.

> Fortune in its many forms was seen as a cord, or bond, or fetter, fastened upon a man by higher powers. The etymology of αναγκη, usually translated "necessity" is, says Onians, uncertain, but a connection with αγχειν, "to strangle," has been suggested, relating directly to the idea of a binding cord [...] coming to this image from the other direction, we see that the Latin *expedit* – "it profits," "is advantageous" had an original meaning of "it unfetters." And under an obligation for debt in Roman law was described as bound *nexys*; while property held subject to any such legal obligation was described as "*nexum*". When paid, such a debt was said to have been loosed – *luo, salvo*. A doomed man was *fatis debitus*.[49]

---

[47] WINTERBOURNE, A., *When the Norns have Spoken: Time and Fate in Germanic Paganism*, 93

[48] Ibid.

[49] Ibid.

Fate cannot be understood as a simple chronological event. Fate, like a law or verdict, is something which is pronounced and binds or fetters an individual to their destiny. This is apparent even in an examination of the English word 'fate' which is derived from the Latin *fātum*, past participle of *fāri* (to speak, to say), which indicates a close semantic link to speech and words; 'fate', etymologically described, is something spoken.[50] Likewise, 'destiny' is derived from Latin *dēstinātus*, past participle of the verb *dēstināre*, 'to determine, to make firm', revealing something akin to a law or decision giving shape and structure to events.[51] It is not simply a chronological event – fate and destiny are concepts which are decided and pronounced.

Ørlog, in light of fate being seen as a type of cosmic law, passes very close to the Hindu concepts of *dharma* and *ṛta*. The best way in which to describe ṛta is perhaps to adopt Louis Renou's definition, "ṛta, which for convenience sake be translated by order (cosmic order and moral order) or by law, is, more precisely, the result of correlations, the product of 'adaption,' of the 'fitting together' between the microcosm and the macrocosm." In this way ṛta can be seen as a force of the expression of an activity which we would call the law of transformation, as is contained in the very root of the word itself √ṛ which means to 'move, to go'.

---

[50] BEK-PEDERSON, J., *The Norns in Old Norse Mythology*, 166

[51] Ibid.

Dharma—or more correctly *dharman*—differs slightly from the concept of ṛta, in the regard that whilst ṛta is an undeniable expression of cosmic truth and order, dharman is its manifestation on the abstract and conceptual plane – it is the social code that reflects the higher truth of the macrocosmic order onto the microcosm. Through the establishment of laws, this is enacted on the socio-ethical plane, and as an expression of truth, *satya-dharman* manifests in human society as social order and human relationships – *satya* (truth) as related to society becomes dharma. In early Vedic texts, dharman refers to an established or proper mode of conduct that supports or helps maintain the continuing health of the world, with Vedic seers describing dharman as the pillar that props up the universe. Over time, both ṛta and dharman fell out of popular usage, being replaced by the word dharma, which is still in use today.

The notion of karma which implies the setting right of any wrong action, the bringing back into harmony of what has been disharmonious, discordant, out of tune or out of order, is contained in the root idea of ṛta, in as much as ṛta stands for harmony and orderly process, that right working of all things and the inherent law of the universe which is the basis of manifestation, its opposite, is said to be punished by the Gods who have taken their stand on the side of the cosmic order.[52] Thus, ṛta itself is a form of fate, which has predestined events from the

---

[52] TAUNTON, G., *The Tantric Traditions: Gods, Rituals, &*

beginning and impacts on both dharma/dharman and individuals alike.

In regard to the knowledge of the Nornir concerning future events and possible issues which could arise from their decisions, one would have to assume that they also possess knowledge of contingent events, i.e. events that may or may not occur based on their decision. Presumably, the verdicts of the Nornir are also not random, and even though consequences are not apparent to mortals, decisions passed by the Nornir were done so in order to ensure that the cosmic law or cycle of events proceeded in accordance to their plans. Interestingly enough, in order for any form of divination to be accurate, this theory must hold true since only an event which was already predestined to occur could be predicted. This would still allow for a modicum of free will, but nonetheless an accurately predicted fate would occur anyway—which is what we see when an outcome foretold by the Gods occurs in a convoluted manner—by the false interpretation of a riddle, or by the vain attempt to take a course of action that will defeat the oracle.[53]

Since the Nornir are regarded as somewhat ambivalent but not deliberately malicious, we have

---

Esoteric Teachings in the Kali Yuga (Australia: Manticore Press, 2018), pp. 132-133

[53] For any form of divination or oracular knowledge to be possible, it cannot occur without predestination, which results in issues arising from the philosophical concept of 'free will' in Tradition.

to assume that their verdicts are always passed in the name of the greater good, even if it results in the outright destruction of an individual's life. The Nornir are not entirely cold in their judgment, but as a cosmic power the importance of an individual is significantly less than that of achieving the 'greater good'. As we see below in this extract from *Atlakviða*, sometimes the Nornir are shown to express sadness at the judgment they themselves have been forced to pass.

> It were better, brother,
> If you had come in armor,
> Like hearth-encircling helmets,
> To see Atli's home
> Had you sat in the saddle
> Through sun-heated days,
> Made the Nornir weep
> At corpses deathly pale.[54]

---

[54] These are the myths featuring the motif of 'futile precautions.'

MAGIC: THE WEB OF WORDS

> Svipdagr I am called,
> Sólbiartr my father was called,
> I came hence on wind-cold roads,
> The words of Urðr
> No man can hinder,
> Though it was flawed in its creation.
> - *Fjolsvinnsmal*[55]

One popular image that persists in regards to both the Nornir and the Moirai is the idea that they 'spin' threads, and that these threads represent the lives of mortals. The Nornir are often shown in this manner and are depicted as three maidens of varying age, weaving or spinning threads. As we see illustrated in the passage below from *Njal's Saga*, even the lives involved in combat and the outcome of the war itself is depicted as woven, and human life itself is the fabric of which fate is composed.

> A wide warp
> Warns of slaughter;
> Blood rains
> From the beam's cloud.
>
> A spear-grey fabric
> Is being spun,

---

[55] BEK-PEDERSON. J., *The Norns in Old Norse Mythology*, 13

Which the friends
Of Randver's slayer
Will fill out
With red weft.

The warp is woven
With warriors' guts
And heavily weighted
With the heads of men.
Spears serve as heddle rods,
Spattered with blood;
Iron bound is the shed-rod,
And arrows are the pin beaters;
We will beat with swords
Our battle web.[56]

Though spinning is referred to here in the English translation of *Njal's Saga* and the Nornir are not referenced directly, actual references to the Nornir spinning are somewhat more complex. The word *ørlǫgþátto* (fate threads) are often found accompanied by such verbs as *snúa* (to twist), *greiða* (to comb out, arrange), and *bregða*, (to braid, throw across).[57] If the intention was to unequivocally portray fabric spinning, one would have expected the verb *spinna* to be employed.[58] Furthermore,

---

[56] BEK-PEDERSON. J., *The Norns in Old Norse Mythology*, 183

[57] WINTERBOURNE, A., *When the Norns have Spoken: Time and Fate in Germanic Paganism*, 98

[58] BEK-PEDERSON. J., *The Norns in Old Norse Mythology*, 129

in some of the depictions, a plying of thread is indicated as opposed to an image of spinning. This would make sense if each Norn held a strand of the fate of a single individual and braided them together to shape the future. It is clear that the Nornir are connected with textile symbolism though, even if it does not involve the commonly accepted motif of spinning.

The earliest known point of reference for a connection between textile work and the Nornir is in *Darraðarljóð* and a number of scholars have interpreted the poem as evidence for this link, such as Holtsmark.[59] It is also claimed that the symbolism of spinning is connected to the Indo-European root *ner* (twist, wind), and possibly the Swedish dialect word *norna* (*nyrna*), a verb which means 'secretly communicate.'[60] The fact that the word Nornir may be related to both these terms is interesting, for there is a connection between the concept of fate and destiny not being 'fixed' until a final verdict is voiced or pronounced. Therefore, there is a link between the Nornir and the evocative power of the spoken word. The connection between fate and the spoken word is also seen in portrayals of the Goddess Frigg, who despite having full knowledge of fate, never speaks of it. This is illustrated by the *Lokasenna* where Freyra states the following: "*ørlog Frigg hygg ec at oll viti, þótt hon sjálfgi segi*" (Frigg,

---

[59] BEK-PEDERSON. J., *The Norns in Old Norse Mythology*, 129

[60] Ibid., 138

I think, knows all fate, though she herself does not speak).⁶¹ Frigg has knowledge of fate which is similar to that which is possessed by the Nornir. She remains silent about her knowledge, not because of modesty or fear, but because by 'voicing' it, her words will seal fate. Until the moment it is vocally announced fate has not been determined.

The notion of fate needing to be pronounced prior to its becoming a concrete temporal event is also found in the Hellenic counterparts of the Nornir, the Moirai. In the extract below, fate is related to truth, in a similar manner as fate was to the law in the case of the Nornir, which lends further impetus to the hypothesis that both the Moirai and the Nornir have a similar function to the Hindu ṛta.

> The Alexandrian Hyginus, a librarian of the Palatine, produced a mythological history, wherein he attributes to the Greek Fates the invention of the first five letters of the alphabet. This is an interesting concept in this context since it introduces a link that will be affirmed throughout what follows, *viz.* that between fate and words (truth), rather than fate and time. The Latin forms fatum, *fata* – "that which is spoken" (from *fari* = speak) appear to be etymologically related to the Greek Moirai.⁶²

---

[61] BEK-PEDERSON. J., *The Norns in Old Norse Mythology*, 191

[62] Ibid., 57

A demonstration of how fate can be 'fixed' in a verbal manner is found in a passage from *Gautrekssaga*, concerning Starkaðr. There is an interesting incident where Oðinn and Thôrr decide his fate, through what can only be described as a 'weaving of words', with one assuming the role of a benefactor, the other an adversary. This serves as a prime example of fate being verbally designated.

> The *Gautrekssaga* tells us (Fornald. Sög. 3, 32), that at midnight Hrosshârsgrani awoke his foster-son Starkaðr, and carried him in his boat to an island. There, in a wood, eleven men sat in council; the twelfth chair stood vacant, but Hrosshârsgrani took it, and all saluted him as Oðinn. And Oðinn said the demsters should deem the doom of Starkaðr (*dômendr skyldi dœma örlug St.*). Then spake Thôrr, who was wroth with the mother of the lad: I shape for him, that he have neither son nor daughter, but be the last of his race. Oðinn said: I shape him, that he live three men's lifetimes (conf. Saxo Gram. p. 103). Thôrr: in each lifetime he shall do a '*niðings-verk.*' Oðinn: I shape him, that he have the best weapons and raiment. Thôrr: he shall have neither land nor soil. Oðinn: I give him, that he have store of money and chattels. Thôrr: I say unto him, that he take in every battle grievous wounds. Oðinn: I give him the gift of poetry. Thôrr: what he composes he shall not be able to remember. Oðinn: this I shape

him, that he be prized by the best and noblest men. Thôrr: by the people he will be hated. Then the deemsters awarded to Starkaðr all the doom that was deemed, the council broke up, and Hrosshârsgrani and his pupil went to their boat.[63]

There is also a strong link between the spoken word and the art of magic, so the process of speaking the fate of another is, in fact, a magical act which binds or fetters the target to the pronounced verdict or destiny. Modern Icelandic has two compound nouns that distinguish between, on the one-hand, *örlaganornir*, 'fate-nornir', and, on the other hand, *galdranornir*, 'witch-nornir' and *töfranornir*, 'sorcery-nornir'.[64] The fact that the words connected with magic, sorcery, and witchcraft are found paired with the name of the Nornir, is highly suggestive of the fact that when the Nornir are pronouncing fate they do not weave a physical yarn, but rather the term is a metaphor for a 'tapestry of words', and the language is used and 'woven' via a magical process. Their counterparts Moirai and the Parcae are also referred to as *fata* (plural of *fatum*) meaning prophetic declaration, oracle, or destiny. The English words fate (wyrd) and fairy (magic, enchantment), are both derived from fata/fatum, which demonstrates that in the English language at

---

[63] WINTERBOURNE, A., *When the Norns have Spoken: Time and Fate in Germanic Paganism*, 85

[64] BEK-PEDERSON. J., *The Norns in Old Norse Mythology*, 2

least, there is a clear connection between fate and magic.

Magic itself as an esoteric art form has a long and vibrant history which connects itself to the power of oral communication. Originally magic referred to the wisdom of the Eastern mystics (*magus* or *magi,* denoting members of the Persian priestly class). The word is probably derived from the Sanskrit *magha* which means not only a class of people, but 'great wealth' endowed by the chief of the Gods Indra, who possess it in plenty, hence why he is called Maghavān). The word magha is cognate with *mahat* (from *maghash*), which means undifferentiated consciousness or ego, *ahamkāra*, and objective consciousness or *manas*).[65] Magic is thus actually an aspect of knowledge which concerns consciousness and seeks to understand the dynamics of consciousness, to train consciousness and apply it to secure personal and collective welfare. Whilst any further elaboration on the nature and theory of magic is outside of the scope of this essay, parts of the mechanism involved in the use of magic need to be examined in order to fully understand the nature of the Nornir and the hidden operations behind the 'spinning of fate'. Firstly, it helps to take into account Wax's point that magic can function "only in an environment where the gods or other powers are sensitive to sanctions, where they can be moved, impressed, bribed, or even threatened, by

---

[65] RAMACHANDRA RAO, S. K., *The Yantra: Text with 32 Plates*, (India: Sri Satguru Publications), 2

the prayers, repentance, good deeds, and sacrifices of men […] If the supreme power is conceived of as impersonal and immutable, magic of any variety becomes a futility".[66] This implies that the very act of magic itself is dependent on a sentient power which can direct fate—which would in return make the Nornir strongly linked to the operations of magic—for without their consent a magically constructed event could not occur. The most important aspect of this, the magic power of the Nornir, is also connected to words, for as we saw earlier, fate is not fixed until it is pronounced. The true magical act of the Nornir lies not in the spinning, but in the art of the spoken word.

POETIC MEAD AND NUMINOUS POWER

I say that one must be a seer, make oneself a seer. The poet becomes a seer through a long, immense, and reasoned derangement of all the senses.
– *Arthur Rimbaud*

The power inherent in the spoken and written word has been a component of magic since the beginnings of history, and it is no less prominent now than it

---

[66] WINTERBOURNE, A., *When the Norns have Spoken: Time and Fate in Germanic Paganism*, 113

was a millennium ago. Whilst we no longer connect it to occult prowess in the modern era, the power of language is certainly no less important now than it was then. The subliminal effects of language upon the nature of conscious and subconscious thought are still studied in philosophy and cognitive science. Regardless of belief in magic, language is the medium by which thoughts and events are connected, as is mentioned in this extract which demonstrates the philosophical principles behind words and language.

> Word introduces discontinuity into experience. Word presents itself as other and remains the other even when heard and recognized. Fixed in its otherness it returns to itself. It does not lend towards other terms, it does not provoke movement. It offers itself in its unity with neither relation nor connexion – a unity which must be taken in its closeness […] Word is linked to event, it itself is event.[67]

Even in contemporary theories on the use of language, words are linked to events—and given this association still exists today, it is by no means a stretch of the imagination to assume that there is a link between verbally pronouncing an event and it transpiring. In the theories related to magic, language represents the transition point

---

[67] LADRIERE, J., *Language & Belief* (Ireland: Gill and MacMillan, 1972), 175

between subject and object—the power of speech draws the desired goal of ritual towards a physical manifestation. The word is the instrument of the will. As such, the word represents a term sent forth by the speaker as his delegate, as it were, his presence sent outside himself – the word is the magical operative for the external condition.[68]

The oral component has a long and arduous history in religious thought, beginning with the *Rig Veda*, which is alleged to be the voice of the Goddess Vac (Speech). Indeed, the ṛṣi who composed the Vedic texts were also blessed with great oratory skills, performing a triple function of priest, poet, and seer. Words—spoken or written—possess powers which are a fine craft, to be used at will by those who are skilled in composition. The magical use and implementation of alphabetic characters is found in most Traditions and is a hallmark of the esoteric arts. When dealing with the oral ritual components, language is the bridge between the twin poles of cognitive experience, the subject and the object, the real and ideal. When used effectively, it is a tool to focus the will into manifestation – careful use of constructed formulas will enhance this talent. In regard to the Vedas, the power of the spoken word is paramount, for the *Rig Veda* is said to be created by the Goddess Vac, who empowered the Vedic seers to transcribe her words.

---

[68] LADRIERE, J., *Language & Belief*, 177

I move with the Rudras, with the Vasus, with the Adityas and all the gods. I carry both Mitra and Varuna, both Indra and Agni, and both of the Asvins. I carry the swelling soma, the Tvastr, and Pusan and Bhaga. I bestow wealth on the pious sacrificer who presses the soma and offers oblation. I am the queen, the confluence of riches, the skillful one who is first among those worthy of sacrifice. The Gods divided me up into many parts, for I dwell in many places and enter into many forms. The one who eats food, who truly sees, who breathes, who hears what is said, does so through me. Listen, you whom they have heard: what I tell you should be heeded. I am the one who says, by myself, what give joy to Gods and men. Whom I love I make awesome; I make him a sage, a wise man, a Brahmin. I stretch the bow for Rudra so that his arrow will strike down the hater of prayer. I incite the contest among the people. I have pervaded sky and earth. I gave birth to the father on the head of this world. My womb is in the waters, within the ocean. From there I spread out over all creatures and touch the very sky with the crown of my head. I am the one who blows like the wind, embracing all creatures. Beyond the sky, beyond this earth, so much have I become in my greatness.[69]

---

[69] DONIGER O'FLAHERTY, W., trans., *The Rig Veda* (UK: Penguin Books Ltd, 1981), 63

From this hymn it is apparent that Vac (representing Speech) is a good deal more than a mere personification of a natural force, as many Vedic Gods are currently deemed to be – Vac is clearly an abstract embodiment of the creative power in words and language (which is why the 'authorship' of the *Rig Veda* is sometimes attributed to her). She is not just speech, but the primordial power of sound and words – and personifies their ability to create and to influence the course of history. This emphasis on speech or on words is by no means an isolated event in the world of Tradition, and a similar notion is also found in the *Corpus Hermeticm*.

> God has endowed man beyond all mortal creatures with these two gifts: Nous and Speech, both as much valued as immortality. If he uses these gifts rightly, he will be no different from the immortals, and on departing from the body he will be guided by both to the realm of the gods and the blessed ones […] For Agathos Daimon, the blessed god, has said that the soul is in the body, *Nous* in Soul, and the Word in Nous, and that God is the father of these […] The Word is an image of Nous, and Nous is an image of God; just as the body is an image of an idea, and the idea is an image of the soul.[70]

---

[70] MAHÉ, J. P., SALAMAN, C., VAN OYEN, D., WHARTON, W. D., (trans.), *The Way of Hermes: The Corpus Hermeticum/The Definitions of Hermes Trismegistus to Asclepius* (UK: Duckbacks, 2001), 77

Obviously, the idea of the Word being connected to God is also very similar to the concept of Christ as the Logos or Word, which relates to the God of Judeo-Christian mythology. Similar content is also to be found within other Middle Eastern Traditions and Egypt. The Babylonian *Enuma Elish* mentions a time before Gods, names, and speech existed, which has a magico-religious function related to it.

> "When yet no Gods were manifest, / Nor names pronounced, nor destinies decreed, / Then Gods were born within them. Lahmu [and] Lahamu emerged, their names pronounced." […] Related to this is the fact that within all mythologies there is an intimate connection between speech and magic [...] as far back as ancient Egypt the hieroglyph for 'spell' was a mouth – where the word for the former was '*rw*'.[71]

The importance of language also appears in the Northern Traditions in the guise of the poetic mead, which has qualities in common with the Vedic *soma*. Not only is the poetic mead clearly linked to Oðinn, it is also linked to power and sovereignty, as well as having an obvious association with the spoken word via poetry. In the Northern Traditions, the emphasis was also placed on the importance of words, which helped to shape an image of their own reality.

---

[71] WINTERBOURNE, A., *When the Norns have Spoken: Time and Fate in Germanic Paganism*, 86

> Great influence over the various affairs of life was attributed to the spoken word. The effect of a spoken sentence could not be questioned and could never be taken back – almost as if it took on physical form, it was there as something absolute. It could only be counteracted through equally strong words. Strong and powerful words appear throughout the saga literature. Words created reality – not just the other way round.[72]

The divine and numinous power of the word is ecstatic in its full manifestation and can only be truly expressed via altered states of consciousness,[73] hence its association with powerful intoxicants like soma. Pronounced in a certain manner, language passes from the subjective state, acting as a medium by which to bring an event into the physical state of reality, thus representing the transitional boundary between the subject and the object. This is the root of its magical potency, the spoken word is the catalyst which brings theoretical acts into the realm of the material and is the mechanism by which the magi annunciate their will. Thus, spinning is not the true magic of the Nornir, they are weaving a web of

---

[72] BEK-PEDERSON. J., *The Norns in Old Norse Mythology*, 190

[73] This is not an endorsement for any type of intoxication other than the 'nectar of the divine'. Though poets have obviously used physical intoxicants during history, the full power of prophecy does not require any form of artificial stimulus which is not of spiritual origin.

magic, a tapestry of words in which the warp and weft of threads become a metaphor for human lives, and the braiding of yarn is the fate they pronounce, becoming fixed once declared. Spinning a tale, or telling a yarn – these are common euphemisms that can be found all throughout the English language. The crafts associated with textiles have often been utilized as a metaphor for speech – and in the specific case of the Nornir, it is *magical speech* which bends the destiny of man to the will of the Gods.

THE WELL OF WYRD

The poetic mead is not an exact equivalent to Urðarbrunnr,[74] but there is a level of correspondence nonetheless. The mead clearly relates to Mímisbrunnr with its connotations of wisdom and knowledge and as the object of Oðinn's quest in *Völuspá*, where he seeks out Mímisbrunnr to get counsel from Mímir. Thus, Oðinn seeks out three liquids with similar intentions: Mímisbrunnr in *Völuspá* and *Glyfaginning*; and Urðarbrunnr and Gunnloð's mead in *Hávamál*.[75] Urðarbrunnr is presided over by the Nornir, implying that the knowledge which flows from their well is something which Oðinn does not naturally possess. Yggdrasill

---

[74] Old Norse for 'Well of Urðr'.

[75] BEK-PEDERSON. J., *The Norns in Old Norse Mythology*, 103

also draws sustenance from this well, and one of its three roots is cited as being in Urðarbrunnr. According to Snorri Sturluson, "It is also said that the Norns that dwell by Weird's well take water from the well each day and with it the mud that lies round the well and pour it up over the ash so that its branches may not rot or decay".[76] This suggests that the water of Urðarbrunnr has mystical life-giving properties. Even so, the water of Urðarbrunnr does not have the power to curtail the destructive forces of Ragnarök for it states in *Forspjallsljod*, "that Urðr's Odrcerir (Urðr's fountain) did not have sufficient power to supply protection against the terrible cold."[77]

One extract from *Völuspá* not only contains mention of Yggdrasill drawing nourishment from Urðarbrunnr, it also contains a reference to an image connected to the Nornir, 'being carved on slips of wood'. Some people have taken this as primary evidence for the runes being used as a tool for divination. Whilst there is little surviving evidence to support the traditional use of runes as a tool for oracles, most languages have a system of alphabetic characters for this purpose – which again would tie language to magic (in the form of divination) and it would be natural for divination to be associated with the Nornir. As was pointed out earlier, in order for any form of divination to be successful,

---

[76] BEK-PEDERSON. J., *The Norns in Old Norse Mythology*, 92

[77] KERÉNYI. C., *The Gods of the Greeks*, 119

predestination has to exist as a matter of logic, even if it still allows for a amount of 'free will'.

> I know an ash that stands
> Called Yggdrasill,
> A tall tree, watered
> With white silt;
> From there come the dews
> That fall in the valleys;
> It stands eternally, green
> Over the well of Urðr.
>
> From there come maidens,
> Knowledgeable of many things,
> Three, from that lake
> Which stands under the tree;
> One they called Urðr,
> Another called Verðandi,
> They carved on slips of wood –
> Skuld the third one.
> They laid down laws,
> They chose life
> For the children of men,
> The fate of men.[78]

What is especially interesting is that this translation appears to associate the runes[79] with Skuld. This again indicates that the Nornir do not possess

---

[78] BEK-PEDERSON. J., *The Norns in Old Norse Mythology*, 75

[79] If this is what is meant by 'slips of wood'.

a primarily chronological function. If they did, all three would be involved, but only Skuld is associated with the runes here. This is because she represents 'debt' which results from human actions that are allocated in the prior two sequential stages of destiny by Urðr and Verðandi.

CONCLUSION

> You mistress Moira, and Tyche, and my Daemon.
> - *Euripides*

Given the complexities surrounding the Nornir, such as the use of different terms for fate, it is apparent that they are not merely personifications of time. The common interpretation of the Nornir as Past, Present, and Future is far too simplistic and runs contrary to the evidence presented here. Likewise, the juridical and magical functions of the Nornir are not explained by this attribution of chronology to the Norns. The Nornir do not merely weave threads, they are 'spinning words' into a web of fixed magical properties, with the aspects of one's individual fate only becoming actualized once it is 'pronounced' by the Nornir, presumably with Skuld having the final word. The evidence for this is also apparent in their connections to terms related to magic, language, and legislative processes. With the exception of Oðinn himself, the Nornir have complete mastery over the spoken word, their words shape the warp and weft of destiny, and they do not merely transcribe reality – the Nornir write reality.

The Nornir are a Tripartite Goddess which is representational of Divine or Cosmic Order, and 'time' is just a basic subsidiary of this wider function. The linguistic connections between the different terms for fate, suggest the way the three 'strands' function is more closely aligned with the Hindu concepts of ṛta/dharman/karma. Actions fated from the beginning, and present actions which may or may not be in accordance with what Urðr decrees. If the actions prescribed by the second Nornir are in concord with the first, the 'karma' will be good. If not, then Skuld will ensure the 'debt' is paid in full. Obviously, the sinister side of Skuld would naturally become more apparent if she is the personification of a 'cosmic debt collector' and it is her task to decide the future. The sequence of the Nornir would still, therefore, be linear, passing from Urðr to Verðandi, and lastly to Skuld, who is the one who decides the final end of a mortal.

The image of a triple Goddess controlling fate appears to be a very widespread belief, and at first glance it would appear to be one of Indo-European origin. There is no evidence of a Tripartite Goddess operating in this manner in India, which is evidence enough to dismiss the Nornir as having a Indo-European origin. The interesting aspect is that this figure of the Goddess is found in Greece, Rome, and other regions of Europe, which does suggest that it is part of a religious genus that migrated through the Mediterranean and Europe. As no evidence of the Nornir can be found predating the Romans, the most logical explanation is that the Romans, on their missions of conquest and on trade routes through Northern Europe, spread the worship of the Parcae through Europe; the Parcae themselves being a derivative of the Greek Moirai. It is well known that much of Roman religion was syncretized with the Hellenic Tradition. The import of the Parcae was then overlaid onto an older concept in which fate was not personified, but was purely an intellectual abstraction, as is indicated by the different terms and phrases for fate. The idea of fate in the Northern Traditions appears to be present in a similar fashion to the Vedic theories on the interplay between destiny and human action, resulting in the consequences of karma, which is referred to as 'debt'. The older form of abstraction, which had a function of explaining the idea of predestination, was gradually merged with the Parcae/Moirai whose worship was spread in Europe via the Romans. This would explain the lack of evidence in India, where the concept has remained more philosophical and has not been anthropomorphized. It is also probable that the premise of the ṛta/dharma/karma trinity is also of Proto-Indo-European origin, and that in some regions it was personified and in others it was not. This would not explain why it is always represented as a trinity of female figures, however, so the conclusion rests on the hypothesis that the Nornir represent ṛta/dharma/karma or cosmic order/prescribed actions/debt, and that their depiction as a Tripartite Goddess evolved from contact with the Roman civilization.

Ultimately, what has happened in the formation of the Nornir is that a very old concept of the creative interplay betwixt time, fate, and divine law as an attempt to explain predestination, was gradually combined with a similar Tradition in which the principle of fate had been anthropomorphized into a Tripartite Goddess, who became the Nornir as we know them today.

PART II

THE TWILIGHT OF THE GODS

AN EXEGESIS OF VÖLUSPÁ

THE END OF THE WORLD. IT IS THE ULTIMATE *mysterium tremendum et fascinans* which serves to both fascinate and terrorize us. The events which lead to the final Armageddon span the eons, at the end of which nothing remains but the final embrace of pure annihilation. From the beginning of time tales of cataclysms have always served to enchant the imagination, as well as to perpetuate fear that the 'end is nigh.' Epic and potent in their flow of discourse, apocalypse myths are complicated by two factors. Firstly, they should not be regarded as extraneous from the larger part of the mythic corpus – meaning that they need to be studied within the broader religious context, for it is only by viewing the final stage as the culmination of a sequence of prior events within the larger cycle that events such as Ragnarök can be correctly interpreted. The second problem lies in the interpretive analysis itself – to what extent can events be read as literal, and which aspects should be regarded as allegorical? The most sensible option is to adopt a balanced approach, and improbable events should be interpreted as metaphorical, whilst feasible ones can be reasonably inferred to as relating to physical events.

Ragnarök refers to the doom or final destiny of the Gods. Jacob Grimm provides a synopsis of Ragnarök when he describes it as the "winding-up of a fuller representation of the end of the world, whose advent is named *aldar rök, aldar lug, aldar rof*, but more commonly *ragna rök* or *ragna rökr* (*Rök* and *rökr* both mean darkness), *rök rökra* [...] is an intensified expression of utter darkness."[1] By the time Ragnarök concludes, almost every figure featured in the narrative will be dead, and the cycle of time shall begin anew.

When examined from the perspective of perennial philosophy, it can be seen that Ragnarök has cognates within the Traditions of many other cultures. Its equivalent in Hinduism is the moment of final dissolution at the end of the Kali Yuga. In Hindu Tradition the Yugas (or Ages) begin with the Satya, from which there is a cycle of gradual decline in morality and the quality of life until the end of the Kali Yuga is reached – at which point the world is purified through destruction and returns to the Golden Age. This exact same process is found in the Northern Traditions as the Axe Age, the Sword Age,

---

[1] GRIMM, J., *Teutonic Mythology, Vol. IV* (New York: Dover Publications, 2004), 813.

Wind Age, and Wolf Age. The end of the Wolf Age is the culmination of Ragnarök. It has also previously been compared to the Christian apocalypse contained in the Book of Revelations. The theory that the two are connected is due to the Christian incursion into Europe which led to the almost complete obliteration of its indigenous traditions. This, unfortunately, also led to a Christian influence over all scholastic endeavors involving the native religion. Naturally, this influence has also raised the question as to how much credibility can be attached to the interpretations of Christian scholars, for one must question their motivations. Are the Eddas and the tales of the North stained by the beliefs of the Christians who transcribed them? How much integrity can we actually place on the surviving texts from this era?

In order to answer these questions, one has to compare the Northern Traditions to another religion, namely that of Hinduism, to fill in any gaps in knowledge which have occurred from either deliberate omission or negligent transcriptions. As primary material which presents an in-depth study of the Northern Traditions is scarce, myths which are said to occur prior to Ragnarök will be examined to facilitate understanding of the event. By demonstrating the connection to tales that precede Ragnarök chronologically, the myth of Ragnarök will be shown to be free from Christian influence, and is an Indo-European concept.

THE COSMIC CYCLE

> In the Winning Age, religion is entire, standing on all four feet, and so is the truth; and men do not acquire any gain through irreligion. But in the other (Ages), through such wrong gained, religion is brought down foot by foot; and because of theft, lying, and deceit, religion goes away foot by foot.
> – *The Laws of Manu*

According to perennial philosophy, the various epochs of human history are represented by a cycle of ages, each of which deteriorates in a state of gradual degeneration. Within the Hellenic Tradition, they are described as the Five Ages in Hesiod's *Works & Days*. In the Roman Tradition, this is reduced back down to four by Ovid in *Metamorphoses*. In regard to the differing number of Ages, it is possible that the Heroic Age is a subdivision of the Bronze Age, since unlike the others, it is not named after a metal, and thus appears to be separate. The Ages are respectively entitled as the Gold, Silver, Bronze, Heroic, and Iron, with each epoch succumbing to increased entropy. In Hinduism, this process is known as the Four Yugas, respectively titled the Satya (or Krta Yuga), Tretā Yuga, Dvāpara Yuga, and the Kali Yuga. These Four Ages are part of a greater cycle of existence, known in Hinduism as a

Manvantāra. Unlike the Hindu Tradition, no dates are provided for the duration of the cycles, and textual references to the Nordic cycle are scarce, which can most likely be attributed to the loss of their texts during the period of Christian hegemony. Similar versions of this myth are also found in the Chaldean, Egyptian, Aztec, and Nordic Traditions. In Hinduism the gradual process of degeneration between the cycles is represented by the Bull of Dharma, which progressively loses its footing as the ages pass and moral degeneration progresses, until unable to stand, the bull finally collapses. The North European cognates are the Axe, Sword, Wind, and Wolf Ages.

The Axe Age is the first cited of these ages and is virtually identical to both the Hindu Satya Yuga and the Greek Golden Age. *The Elder Edda of Saemund Sigfusson* even provides a direct reference to the Golden Age:

> "In the beginning," answered Har, "he appointed rulers, and bade them judge with him the fate of men, and regulate the government of the celestial city. They met for this purpose in a place called Idavoll, which is in the center of the divine abode. Their first work was to erect a court or hall wherein are twelve seats for themselves, besides the throne which is occupied by the All-Father. This hall is the largest and most magnificent in the universe, being resplendent on all sides, both within

and without, with the finest gold. Its name is Glaðsheimr. They also erected another hall for the sanctuary of the Goddesses. It is a very fair structure and called by men Vingolf. Lastly, they built a smithy and furnished it with hammers, tongs, and anvils, and with these made all the other requisite instruments, with which they worked in metal, stone, and wood, and composed so large a quantity of the metal called gold that they made all their movables of it. Hence that age was named the Golden Age. This was the age that lasted until the arrival of the women out of Jötunheimr, who corrupted it."[2]

The consequence of the first deceitful act was that the smiths refused to serve the Gods any longer, due to the arrival of women from Jötunheimr. Through the arrival of these women, greed is born into the world by the 'women from Jötunheimr'. The artists/craftsmen depart the divine court, displeased with the Gods.[3] The Smiths represent the creative forces in society. The significance of this is two-fold, for if we adopt Dumézil's theory of myth (based on the Indo-European system of caste), this amounts to nothing less than a rebellion of the third caste. The corruption which is spread by the women out of Jötunheimr is the introduction of greed to the

---

[2] THORPE, B., *The Elder Edda of Saemund Sigfusson* (USA: General Books LLC, 2009), 172

[3] RYDBERG, V., *Teutonic Mythology* (USA: General Books LLC, 2009), 100

world, which is equivalent to the European Myth of the Fall, and has cultural parallels all across the globe. In Semitic mythology it corresponds with the myth of Adam and Eve, who fell from grace by lust, and in Greek myth when Prometheus falls from *hybris* – the corresponding 'sin' in the Northern Traditions is to fall from greed. This is the decisive point of decline in the cycle of the Ages, making greed the 'original sin' in the Northern Traditions. It begins with the transformation of gold from being primarily an aesthetic item to a symbol of avarice. Gold is almost exclusively referenced as the solar metal *par excellence*, adding further credence to the fact that the Golden Age, is in fact, the Solar Age – the Sun being the symbol of creative power, honor, and law.

It is also worth noting the solar symbolism of the Gods. There are twelve seats, the number of months which comprise a solar year, and a thirteenth for the All-Father, suggesting the placement of Oðinn's seat as a symbol of sovereignty over the solar year. As the Ages progress, the abstract quality of 'light' present in the higher faculties of humanity decline in correspondence with human morality, until the age of 'darkness' accelerates, and the sun is finally erased from the sky. The waning of light represents the progressive decline of humanity in which all traces of social and moral order have been broken, and is a state of darkness or blindness, which is a metaphor for lack of perception.

FATE & THE TWILIGHT OF THE GODS

BOUND IN BLOOD

> Loki said: "Do you remember, Oðinn, when in bygone days we mixed our blood together? You said you would never drink ale unless it were brought to both of us."
> – *Poetic Edda*

The role of Oðinn in the cycle is extremely significant, for he is the key figure in the prevention and/or forestalling of Ragnarök. Indeed, Ragnarök is seen to be inevitable, and even Oðinn cannot prevent its advent; the only thing to be done is it to forestall it. Because his plans to delay Ragnarök sometimes inflict suffering on mortals and immortals alike, some people regard Oðinn as an untrustworthy deity. In this judgment, however, what they do not realize is that the needs of the many outweigh the needs of the few. Oðinn's dedication to preserving humanity from Ragnarök render him trustworthy in the extreme.

There has been a certain amount of disagreement as to what Oðinn's specific sphere of powers is as a God, for unlike the rest of the Æsir, his role is not clear-cut. A various number of opinions have been voiced. Haugen, for example, groups Oðinn's various capacities from 'patriarch of Gods and man' to 'God of magic' into one complex which could roughly be labeled 'intellectual' and opposes this to the God Thôrr, whom he sees as marked by the single characteristic of strength.[4] Fleck, on the other hand, concentrates on Oðinn's capacity as God of wisdom, and sees this as the key to his position of power in the society of the Gods, providing a detailed account of Oðinn's acquisition of knowledge, and concluding that Oðinn is not merely a repository of wisdom, but rather functions actively as a source of knowledge.[5] What is interesting here, is that the two scholars seem to have established a division between the mental faculties of intelligence and wisdom. As to why the two forms of cognition should be mutually exclusive is mentioned in neither hypothesis, and it is a matter of debate as to whether there is any clear distinction between intelligence and wisdom. Perhaps, in modern terminology, they could be rendered as two different forms of cognitive processes – the EQ (emotional quotient) and the IQ (intellectual quotient). What Oðinn appears to be, however, is an embodiment of higher cognition at a level which has absorbed the functions of other principle deities, to create a manifestation of what could be called a 'gestalt archetype'. This form of archetype is not unique to the Northern Gods; Shiva in Hinduism is also a manifestation of this, in which a single deity rises to a higher position of prominence than other

---

[4] AULD, R., The Psychological and Mythic Unity of the God Odin in *Numen,* Vol. 23, Fasc. 2 (Netherlands: Brill Academic Publishers, 1976), 146

[5] Ibid.

deities by absorbing the very qualities which made the rival Gods popular. This gradual absorption of qualities is, in all likelihood, a process of synthesis from polytheism towards monotheism.

Another aspect of Oðinn's role as the All-Father arises from the division of the Gods into Æsir and Vanir, with the latter being marked by an association with fertility and matriarchy, battle each other to an indecisive standstill. The conflict has a number of possible interpretations, ranging from a gradual syncretism of two religions, to a clash between matriarchal and patriarchal society. The most probable explanation, however, is a conflict between natural and civilizational forces. The opposition depicted here is eerily reminiscent of the dichotomy in Hinduism between *Vana* (nature) and *Grama* (village) i.e. the dyad formed between nature and organized society. Man's psyche is naturally divided between the two states, as desires and impulses fluctuate from one polarity to the other. What is of particular importance in the tale of arrangements betwixt the Æsir and Vanir, is that the agreement reached by them leads to an exchange of hostages, and the creation of a token of their reconciliation. This token is Kvasir, created by the blending of the spittle of both groups of Gods. Kvasir is subsequently killed and his blood is fermented into the mead of poetry, the essence, as it were of synthesis. Communication is, therefore, the unifying principle. The mead is later consumed by Oðinn, who at this time becomes the primary symbol for the integrated synthesis of the two poles, nature and civilization. It is Oðinn, rather than Kvasir, who carries the force of this symbol in Norse mythology because he continues to operate with the Gods after Kvasir dies, and no further mention of the Vanir, except for the hostages given to the Æsir, is made.[6]

Thus, Oðinn again embodies a 'gestalt archetype' which arises out of the synthesis of two opposing elements in the human consciousness; the natural or Dionysian impulse (Vana and Vanir) and the Apollonian impulse towards civilization (Æsir and Grama). It could also be represented as a further argument that the God's intelligence and wisdom can be attributed to his prowess of absorbing and harnessing multiple energies from other currents. As such, it is Oðinn's task to forestall Ragnarök – to which ends he is willing to make sacrifices and bend the rules with a view to achieving the greater good. This is why it is said that to follow Oðinn requires implicit trust in the God and acceptance of the fact that on occasion, one must suffer in the interest of pursuing a higher cause. Ultimately, however, despite Oðinn's superior mental skills, he will meet his end in the jaws of Fenrir, and Oðinn is fully aware of his fate, as we see outlined below in *The Lay of Vafthrudnir*.

---

[6] AULD, R., The Psychological and Mythic Unity of the God Odin in *Numen*, Vol. 23, Fasc. 2, 149

Gagnrad: Much have I journeyed, etc. Which of the Æsir will rule o'er the Gods' possession, when Surtr's fire shall be clenched?

Vafthrudnir: Vidar and Vali will the Gods' holy fanes inhabit, when Surt's fire shall be quenched. Modi and Magni will Miollnir possess, and warfare strive to end.

Gagnrad: Much have I journeyed, etc. What of Oðinn will the life's end be, when the powers perish?

Vafthrudnir: The wolf will the father of men devour; him Vidar will avenge: he his cold jaws will cleave, in conflict with the wolf.[7]

Thus, not only is Oðinn aware of Ragnarök before it occurs, he is also aware of certain details. However, he still fails to realize what the principle cause of Ragnarök will be. This is a key point in the cycle of events, for Oðinn's role in Ragnarök is mirrored by that of his 'shadow' Loki, who is destined to play the role of the antagonist.

Loki is an interesting deity to study, even if only for his shifting nature and complexity of character. In many ways, he can be seen as the mastermind who instigates Ragnarök, as an act of revenge. Certainly, there is more depth to the character of Loki than has been previously been ascribed to him,

---

[7] THORPE, B., *The Elder Edda of Saemund Sigfusson*, 15

and Loki is not the two-dimensional villain that he is often depicted as. The incomplete portrayal of Loki is partially reflected in the absence of a complete record of the northern religions; had all the texts survived we would probably have had a clearer understanding of his role.

Initially, Loki is described as being the son of the giant Farbauti in *The Elder Edda of Saemund Sigfusson,* named Loki or Loptur.[8]

> His mother is Laufey or Nal; his brothers are Byleist and Helblindi. Loki is handsome and well made, but of a very fickle mood, and most evil disposition. He surpasses all beings in those arts called cunning and perfidy.[9]

One characteristic Loki shares with Oðinn then, is that he also embodies a form of intelligence, and like Oðinn he cannot be placed into a neat category or archetypal role. Loki is a figure which is unique to the Northern Traditions. The uniqueness of his character has been a natural attraction for scholars, and the Indo-Europeanist Georges Dumézil, devoted an entire monograph to the nature of Loki, for whom he could find but one existing match within mythology. According to Dumézil, Loki shows a resemblance to Syrdon, a demonic trickster entity from Caucasian legends.

---

[8] THORPE, B., *The Elder Edda of Saemund Sigfusson,* 181
[9] Ibid.

The trickster's mobility in and of itself is value-neutral; it acquires polarity only in concrete manifestations and existential conditions. When assessed positively, the trickster's mobility is construed as non-conformity, disregard for taboos and prescriptions, freedom from the impediment of prejudice. It allows one to overcome social barriers and overturn social hierarchy, brings the possibility of refuting tradition replacing the authority of forefathers with active exploration of contemporaries. It is this aspect that prompted Georges Dumézil to identify Loki and Syrdon [...] The existing social order reacts to the annihilative power of the restless intellect with self-defense, hostility, which makes the mind to channel some, or not infrequently, most of its capabilities towards cunning, deception, intrigue, as well as, when aided by the vulnerability of character, towards mockery, defiance, hatred. The positive assessment of the jester or buffoon as the catalyst of medieval\carnival spirit" (Mikhail Bakhtin) or of temporary status change" in the rites of traditional societies (Victor Turner), has the same origin as well.[10]

If we accept the hypothesis that Loki represents a form of 'restless' intelligence which acts in the service of good or ill, it also seems logical to accept

---

[10] MANIN, Y. I., *The Mythical Trickster: A Study in Psychology and Culture Theory* (Germany: Bielefeld University)

that his non-conformity and rejection of social norms also cast him in the role of being an 'outsider'. The role of outsider archetypes is a complex one, as they fulfill a function within a certain social group, as well as maintaining another function outside of that group. In this regard, the outsider is always a liminal figure. On one hand, they are accepted by society, but the acceptance is always accompanied by a sense of wariness and unease, for by his presence the outsider threatens to disrupt society. They embody the sense of the 'Other' which arouses fear and distrust. In the case of Loki, there are more than just trickster traits present; Loki repeatedly steps over socially defined boundaries and appears to embody not just 'cunning' or 'craftiness', but rather a form of transgressive intelligence that is applied to deconstructing the existing status quo. Loki's status as a liminal entity is present from his birth, for his lineage is that of being half-god and half-giant – in short, an outsider that sits on the boundary of two opposing cultures and thus embodies elements of both. The role of Loki as an outsider archetype is clearly portrayed in *Cegir's Compotation* and *Loki's Altercation*. In this tale Loki slays Fimafengand and is chased into the forest only to return and systematically insult the Gods one by one – the role seems far from accidental on Loki's part and it appears that he is all too aware of the consequences of his actions. This is no accidental slip on the part of Loki; rather it is a calculated act of malice. His motivation is quite obviously that of disrupting the existing social order within the Æsir. During this confrontation, Loki is repeatedly referred to as an 'impure being' – particularly by Thôrr.

> Silence, thou impure being! My mighty hammer, Miollnir, shall stop thy prattling. Hrungnir's bane shall cast thee down to Hel, beneath the gratings of the dead.[11]

This seems to refer to him having low social status, most likely due to the nature of his birth as a child of two different species. Within this tale Loki's aim is not so much to insult the Gods, but rather point out their own failings, and show that they too are also 'impure' – here Loki is not so much playing the role of a villain, but rather that of a misunderstood entity, a liminal one with low social status, lashing out verbally against those who believe themselves superior to him. This section of the dialogue reveals Loki not as a trickster, but rather a Promethean figure of rebellion against the existing social order – and like Prometheus, the Gods will punish Loki for his zealous insubordination. In European consciousness Prometheus becomes the symbol for man's never-ceasing, unremitting, and relentless struggle against fate, against the Gods, defying the laws of the Olympians, though (and this again shows the continuing absurdity) never being successful in this endeavor, which, however, is necessary for the origin of civilized life (the ultimate paradox of rule-

---

[11] THORPE, B., *The Elder Edda of Saemund Sigfusson*, 63

breaking as a rule).[12] At the end of the event, Loki is captured and imprisoned beneath the earth.

> After this Loki, in the likeness of a salmon, cast himself into the waterfall of Franangr, where the Aesir caught him and bound him with the entrails of his son Nari; but his other son, Narfi, was changed into a wolf. Skadi took a venomous serpent and fastened it up over Loki's face. The venom trickled down from it. Sigyn, Loki's wife, sat by, and held a basin under the venom; and when the basin was full, carried the venom out. Meanwhile, the venom dropped on Loki, who shrank from it so violently that the whole earth trembled. The causes of this are what are now called earthquakes.[13]

A variant of this is also found in the *Poetic Edda*—it is also worth noting that the punishment described here is also the same found in another myth—namely that which occurs when Loki is captured for the death of Baldr. The fact that Loki is explicitly connected with earthquakes here seems to indicate a chthonic connection rather than the previously suggested 'fire God' hypothesis, though the possibility of a volcanic connection is not ruled out,

---

[12] KOEPPING, K. P., Absurdity & Hidden Truth: Cunning Intelligence and Grotesque Body Images as Manifestations of the Trickster in *History of Religions*, vol.. 24 no. 3, (USA: The University of Chicago Press, 1985), 197

[13] THORPE, B., *The Elder Edda of Saemund Sigfusson*, pp. 62-63

with Loki as a subterranean fire God. This concept is not unknown in other cultures, as the Hindu cosmic cycles also make mention of a horse under the sea which generates fire, and is clearly a reference to an underwater volcano. In terms of Loki's relations with other Gods, it would explain his relationship with Thôrr, for not only would they compose an opposite pairing in terms of strength and intelligence, they would also be opposed in the sense of sky and earth. There are also suggestions of a chthonic connection to be found in some of Loki's offspring.

> "Loki," continued Har, "has likewise had three children by Angrboða, a giantess of Jötunheimr. The first is the wolf Fenrir, the second Jörmungandr, the Miðgarðr Serpent; the third Hel (Death).[14]

Hel is cast into Niflheim; hence her dominion has clear chthonic connections. Firstly, Niflheim is located below Yggdrasil, under the third root, immediately situating it beneath the ground in relation to the rest of the tree. Secondly, Niflheim seems to be described as a place of cold and darkness, with mist or fog-like qualities. These qualities are the same as that of the Greek dominion of Hades; an underworld realm of the dead which is ghostly, ethereal, dark and cold. The Greek Goddess Gaea, in her role as the Black Earth Mother reigned as a deity of death and the underworld

---

[14] THORPE, B., *The Elder Edda of Saemund Sigfusson*, 181

and possessed twin aspects, and it possible that this is what the half-living, half dead form of the Goddess Hel represents – the life-giving power of the realm above ground and the deathly world of the subterranean. Similarly, Hel is not the only one of Loki's children to hold a chthonic connection – Jörmungandr cannot possibly be anything else but a chthonic figure due to its inherent symbolism.

> According to the *Edda*, a huge serpent, the *Miðgarðs Ormr*, lies coiled around the earth's circumference, *umiörd allra landra*; evidently the ocean. [...] But that 'world-serpent', hateful to all the Gods (*sû er goð fia*, Sæm. 55a) was the child of Loki, and brother to the Fenris-Ûlfr and Hel; he was called Jörmungandr (sn.32), the great, the godlike and like Hel he opens wide his jaws.[15]

Serpents are always symbols of chthonic power, and when depicted devouring their own tail, as we see with Jörmungandr, it is not only an allegory for time, but also that of the earth's rotation. Thus, it is not just time that is symbolized by Jörmungandr, but the measuring of time that comes from the rotation of the earth/Miðgarðr. When Jörmungandr ceases to 'eat' its tail and ascends from the waters, the earth no longer rotates. Obviously, this is a time of great disaster and it, for this reason, the Jörmungandr rises from the waters during Ragnarök.

---

[15] GRIMM, J., *Teutonic Mythology Vol. II*, 794

The third of Loki's offspring is the wolf Fenrir; in contrast to the first two of Loki's offspring who clearly represent chthonic forms of time and death, with Fenrir there also appears to an abstract aspect of morality present, and it is this level of psychological implications that renders Fenrir more complex than its siblings.

In the tremendous battle between the Gods and the creatures of the underworld that transpires in Ragnarök, as reported in the final passages of the *Gylfaginning*, Loki and his progeny are unequivocally situated on the side of the God's opponents.[16]

The previous theory of Loki being connected with fire was first put forward by Jacob Grimm, who assigned Loki the attributes of the God of fire based on an onomastic analogy drawn from the German '*lohe*'.[17] Even though the etymology proved untenable, this image has persisted tenaciously in the public imagination – partially due to Richard Wagner's portrayal of 'Loge' in *Der Ring des Nibelungen*.[18] Sophus Bugge (1889), who, in his efforts to trace Norse gods and myths to Christian prototypes, saw in Loki a variant of the Christian Lucifer.[19] This connection seems

---

[16] VON SCHNURBEIN, S., The Function of Loki in Snorri Sturluson's Edda in *History of Religions* (USA: University of Chicago 2000), 114

[17] Ibid., 122

[18] Ibid.

[19] Ibid.

exceedingly tenuous and somewhat reductionist since although both are portrayed as adversaries, Lucifer and Loki share very few characteristics. Another theory as to the nature of Loki was advanced by Jan de Vries who put forward the notion that Loki was a 'trickster' figure, like those most commonly associated with the myths of North American Indians.[20] The trickster is the culture hero who, through his cunning intelligence goes awry, mediates between Gods and men; has unintended consequences, and vice versa. In relation to the trickster archetype, it is noteworthy that the Greeks use the term *angkylometai* for the intelligence of the trickster, as noted by Kerényi. Prometheus uses an intelligence that is knotted like a sling for trapping animals, which implies that the Titans are too smart for their own good, that they possess an intelligence that traps itself in its own snares.[21] Georges Dumézil also ascribed a psychological function to Loki and considered him to be a product of the mythological imagination attempting to create an incarnation of "impulsive intelligence".[22] What is perhaps the most intriguing examination of Loki is presented by Schjødt who considers the contradictory elements in Loki's development from a helpful assistant

---

[20] VON SCHNURBEIN, S., The Function of Loki in Snorri Sturluson's Edda in *History of Religions*, 113

[21] KOEPPING, K. P., Absurdity & Hidden Truth: Cunning Intelligence and Grotesque Body Images as Manifestations of the Trickster in *History of Religions*, vol. 24 no. 3, 206

[22] VON SCHNURBEIN, S., The Function of Loki in Snorri Sturluson's Edda in *History of Religions*, 113

of the Gods to one of their primary adversaries is parallel to the demise of the world.[23] For Schjødt, Loki becomes an exponent of the increasing malevolence and moral disintegration of the world that ultimately leads to its downfall.[24] From Schjødt's perspective, then, Loki becomes, by virtue of his intermediary function, the quintessential symbol of "the Unnatural."[25] By examining Loki from this angle, he then also conforms with both the trickster and the outsider archetypes. The figure of Loki may also embody the Germanic concept of *sjalfrsjalfum*, where the actor becomes the victim.[26] Endi Welsford's view of the fool or trickster's role in myth also highlights an intriguing point when she states that the paradox of the fool, who not only shows society up for what it really is or seems to be behind the mask of surface pretense, of status and role, and of social game playing, but also infers that the fool is at the same time perceived by every kind of audience as the alter ego of the spectator: "He winks at us and we are delighted at the discovery that we also are gluttons and cowards and knaves."[27] As such, we can see the archetype of the trickster to be an exaggeration of our own folly – the trickster

---

[23] VON SCHNURBEIN, S., The Function of Loki in Snorri Sturluson's Edda in *History of Religions*, 115

[24] Ibid.

[25] Ibid., 116

[26] KOEPPING, K. P., Absurdity *&* Hidden Truth: Cunning Intelligence and Grotesque Body Images as Manifestations of the Trickster in *History of Religions*, vol. 24 no. 3, 192

[27] Ibid., 195

serves as a vestibule for mischievous elements in human nature, which can easily pass from harmless fun to malice, and this is the same impulse embodied by Loki. Loki represents the unrestrained will to mischief and cunning, which crosses the social boundaries of what is acceptable and that which is unacceptable. Welsford also draws parallels between 'body image' and the trickster archetype, as is cited here,

> Contrary to this sameness of body imagery is the variability of expression of "hiding the truth," of feints, deceits, and illusions. This may appear in the mode of sacrifice (as a code about sovereignty) – as with Prometheus as Titan, possibly in Loki (also with emphasis on sovereignty), or with the Vedic Indra-Garuda and the Puranic gods, churning the ocean (both as a mixture of sacrificial and alimentary code and, as with Loki, stronger on the code of immortality than is the case in Greece)—in divinatory and thus random playing—as among the Fon with their trickster Legba (with faint Indo-European comparative hints in the *Mahābhārata* in the game for the female partner of the Pandava brothers and in the riddle games Oðinn and Loki of the knucklebones of Hermes in Greece)—or in the mode of "translator of languages"—as with Ananse of the Ashanti (with echoes in Hermes, mediating heaven and

underworld, or in Loki as spokesman between Gods, giants, and dwarfs.[28]

According to this premise, the intellectual Greek trickster Prometheus shows us the operation of thoughts that hide deceit under the surface of smiling negotiation, and the earthy body trickster shows us the hidden dimension of the naked orifices under the clothing of civilized and rule-governed life. Both reveal a hidden truth, and truth might be nothing more than a cruel joke. By laughing about the cruelty and absurdity of natural and divine laws, man has truly reflected on them, and the reflection liberates, as Gadamer put it, "because it makes us free from that which, if not seen through, would oppress us".[29] In Loki, the character traits of both forms of the trickster are embodied. As an 'outsider' Loki's social interactions display criticism, rebellion, protest against existing structures, against boundaries, against the seriousness of order, and constructs which are socially and ritually acknowledged. To a certain extent, Loki and other trickster figures represent manifestations of the chaos on which order depends to function, but which also must be controlled in order for society to function correctly. With Loki's ascendancy to the position of the 'prime adversary' the existing divisive status quote shifts from a dominance of

---

[28] KOEPPING, K. P., Absurdity & Hidden Truth: Cunning Intelligence and Grotesque Body Images as Manifestations of the Trickster in *History of Religions*, vol. 24 no. 3, 200

[29] Ibid., 214

cosmic order to one of cosmic chaos, inverting the existing power paradigm. Loki, who as an outsider/trickster serves a role in the social order of Asgarð by performing tasks that the other Gods cannot or will not do, initially serves as both a scapegoat and a bearer of impurity, ultimately results in his shift from being a manageable trickster to the prime instigator for the forces of chaos, is ultimately the fault of the Asgarðians themselves, who use Loki as the intermediary for 'impure' actions, but whom they also never fully accept as one of they own because of his outsider, half-caste status.

> The eschatological battle brought about by adherence to laws and oaths, which have to be broken, to retain eternal life (for the Gods), as shown through the actions forced on the half-god Loki, that trickster-demon of the dark whom the Ases and Vanes need to do their deeds of law-breaking, whom they, however, refuse to let share in divine drink, who through apparent boons that the Gods delight in (and which they do need) usher in the final annihilation of the cosmos. If these are the problems of the pole of highest sacredness, then the trickster belongs here.[30]

---

[30] KOEPPING, K. P., Absurdity & Hidden Truth: Cunning Intelligence and Grotesque Body Images as Manifestations of the Trickster in *History of Religions*, vol. 24 no. 3, 203

VÖLUPSÁ – THE VALA'S PROPHECY

> The sun grows dark, / the earth sinks into the sea,
> the bright stars / vanish from heaven,
> smoke rages / with fire,
> the fierce heat plays / upon heaven itself.
> – *Völupsá*[31]

To date, the majority of theories concerning *Völupsá* have dealt with its passage in a very superficial manner and have largely dealt with it's apocalyptic nature, concentrating on natural disasters – by way of example, it has been put forward before that Ragnarök is reminiscent of a volcanic eruption and hence may be Icelandic in origin.[32] Drawing upon the roles of Oðinn and Loki, however, it is possible to provide an alternative explanation for the myth.

The prophecy itself is usually dated to the late tenth century when the native religion was beginning to be replaced by Christianity. It has previously been suggested by scholars that the poem is a sacred text, composed just before their beliefs were eradicated. On the other hand, some scholars have claimed that because of its date and proximity to the rise of Christianity, that it is influenced by Christian

---

[31] CAREY, J., Saint Patrick, the Druids, and the End of the World in *History of Religions,* Vol. 36, no.1 (USA: University of Chicago, 1996), 46

[32] LARRINGTON, C. (trans.), *The Poetic Edda* (UK: Oxford University Press, 1996), xi

eschatology. As far as Christian intervention in the texts of the *Poetic Edda* are concerned, there are passages in which the *Völupsá* directly contradicts Christian teachings, so it is logical to assume that it does preserve indigenous Scandinavian mythology.[33] In addition to this, there is a substantial amount of material which the myth holds in common with Indo-European eschatology, in particular, that of the Greeks and Hindus. A brief summary of the events occurring in *Völupsá* is provided here,

> On this conflict followed the blending of the air with harmful elements, in other words, it was the beginning of the great winter. The first great war in the world breaks out, when Asgarð is stormed and Miðgarðr is covered with battlefields, on which brothers slay each other; Baldr is killed by the mistletoe; the hosts of monsters are born who, in the Iron Wood, await Ragnarök; on account of the sins of men, it became necessary to make places of torture in the lower world. All these terrible events, which happened in time's morning, are the cunning work of the father of misfortunes and of his feminine counterpart.[34]

It seems clear that there is a meteorological event at work here which has a severely negative impact

---

[33] CAREY, J., Saint Patrick, the Druids, and the End of the World in *History of Religions*, Vol. 36, no.1, 46

[34] RYDBERG, V., *Teutonic Mythology*, 101

on the climate. On the metaphorical level, it is also clear that when Baldr is slain, it represents not only the death of the physical sun, but rather the solar aspects which are embodied in humanity; namely creativity, intelligence, and ethics. Thus, the death of Baldr represents the death of higher man. This interior aspect of the decline is ultimately mirrored in the external world by the onset of the Fimbul winter. The collapse of the solar element is found at both the level of intellectual abstraction and in the external environment of Ragnarök. In order to understand the further implications of this, we are required to return to the figure of Loki in order to understand how Ragnarök proceeds. In this regard, there is a significant point which is often overlooked concerning how the myth cycle leading to the conclusion of Ragnarök unfolds. Specifically, this concerns Loki and the death of Baldr.

In the stories which precede Ragnarök, Loki is punished and bound under the mountain for either one of two acts. As was discussed earlier, in the first instance it is a violation of the existing social order and revealing his hidden knowledge, in which Loki becomes a sinister manifestation of the 'fool'. In the second instance, which is the more popular version of the myth, Loki tricks the Gods into slaying Baldr. Knowing that Baldr is invulnerable to all weapons, but can be injured by mistletoe, Loki hands a twig of mistletoe to the blind God Höðr and deceives him into throwing it at Baldr. Once struck by the deadly mistletoe, Baldr 'dies' and enters the realm of Hel. The well-cited explanation here is that the significance of the mistletoe is that it is a plant which blooms in winter; thus its symbolic power to slay the sun God Baldr is easily explained. However, there is another, deeper reason for the power of mistletoe, which has long been buried within the myth, which ties this incident directly to the final days of Ragnarök. Rydberg describes an incident in which a sword named Gamibanteinn is given to Loki by a giant.

> Loki refers to a giant who had given it to him. This word means a weapon made by Volund [...] but is, at the same time, a synonym for *mistelteinn*, hence, in an Icelandic saga from the Christian time, Volund's Sword of Victory also reappears by the name Mistelteinn. Thus the giant gave Loki a weapon, which, according to its designation, is either Volund's Sword of Victory or the Mistletoe. It cannot be the Sword of Victory. We know the hands to which this sword has gone and is to go: Volund's [...] and finally Surtr's. The weapon which Thjasse's namesake Hlebard gives Loki must, accordingly, have been the Mistletoe.[35]

This indicates that there are two powerful swords at play – one representing the conquering potency of the sun, the other a powerful weapon to render the sun impotent. Thus, not only does Loki kill Baldr

---

[35] RYDBERG, V., *Teutonic Mythology*, 146

with mistletoe, he also owns a powerful mystical sword of the same name, which appears to have a connection with the mythical Sword of Victory. The parallel here seems obvious, since, during the incident in which Baldr is slain, the other Gods are throwing weapons at Baldr in jest, knowing that he cannot be armed by then. Under the circumstances, even the blind Höðr would have been able to feel the difference between a twig of mistletoe and weapon, but if he were holding the sword Misteleinn, then he would not have noticed anything unusual. It seems that in the original version of the myth, *Baldr was slain by the magical sword Misteleinn*, and not the plant mistletoe. As for the Sword of Victory, it too plays a role in Ragnarök.

> The Volund Sword – the sword becomes the price of a bride and passes into the hands of the giant Gymer and his wife. Gymer's wife is the same Angrboða who, in historical times and until Ragnarök, dwells in the Iron Wood. Her shepherd, who in the woods watches her monster flocks, also keeps the sword until the fire-giant Fjalar shall appear in his abode in the guise of a red cock and bring it to his own father Surtr, in whose hand it shall cause Freyr's death, and contribute to the destruction of the world of the Gods.[36]

---

[36] RYDBERG, V., *Teutonic Mythology*, 62

Therefore, there are two Volund swords – Mistletoe and the Sword of Victory, one of which passes to Loki, the other to Surtr, both of whom are the primary villains in Ragnarök. The sword which the God Freyr had once possessed, was thereafter, concealed in the earth. Angrboða's shepherd, who again brings the sword into daylight, gives it to Fjalar.[37]

In Roman records, there is also a passage which mentions that the Sword of Victory belongs to Attila the Hun.

> A historian, Priscus, who was Attila's contemporary, relates that the Hun king got a possession of a divine sword that a shepherd had dug out of the ground and presented to him as a gift. The king of the Huns, it is added, rejoiced in the find; for as the possessor of the sword that had belonged to the God "Mars", he considered himself as armed with authority to undertake and carry on successfully any war he pleased (see Jordanes, who quotes Priscus).[38]

The capacity for creating conspiracy myths as to whom now possesses the Sword of Victory are endless, since this passage indicates that the Sword is a physical (as opposed to mythical) object. However, it seems more probable that this version of the myth was purposely revised for use as political

---

[37] RYDBERG, V., *Teutonic Mythology*, 62
[38] Ibid.

propaganda. What is important, however, is the role of Angrboða 'The One Who Brings Grief' or 'She-Who-Offers-Sorrow' and the fire-giant Fjalar.

> "There on a height sat, striking a harp, the giantess's watch, the joyous Egdir; by him crowed, in the bird-wood, the bright red cock, which Fjalar hight".[39] [...] "Crowed o'er the Æsir Gullinkambi, which wakens heroes with the sire of hosts; but another crows beneath the earth, a soot-red cock in the halls of Hel."[40]

The rooster or cockerel is generally considered to be a positive, solar symbol, but can also symbolize pride and arrogance. As the rooster in question here is depicted as being resident in Hel, and of a dark-red color, it seems likely that the cockerel is associated with sunset, and represents the destructive aspect of the solar principle. Additionally, it is Angrboða who dwells in the Iron Wood, and is the mother of Fenrir, Jörmungandr, and Hel. Angrboða is also cited as one of the Thurs-maidens from Jötunheimr. Rydberg describes Angrboða as part of a trinity, but this is a very different group of female figures to that of the ambivalent Nornir.

> Three dangerous Thurs-maidens came from Jötunheimr. These Thurs-maidens are not the Norns, as has usually been assumed [...] the

---

[39] THORPE, B., *The Elder Edda of Saemund Sigfusson*, 7
[40] Ibid., 7

three Thurs-maids are the one who in her unity is triple and is thrice born of different parents. Her name is Heid-Gullveig-Angrboða, and in connection with Loki, she constitutes the evil principle of Teutonic mythology, like Angra Mainyu, and Jahi in the Iranian mythology.[41]

Rather than the Norns, the force most likely at work here is an inversion of the usual trinity of feminine powers. Thus, Rydberg describes her/them as a purely "destructive principle". In view of Angrboða's prominent role in Ragnarök and her relationship with Loki, Angrboða is clearly a malign figure. The three different female beings are just different aspects of the same entity, as is illustrated here,

> She that raw remembers, the first on earth, when Gullveig they with lances pierced, and in the high one's hall her burnt, thrice burnt, thrice brought her forth, oft not seldom; yet she still lives. Heid they called her, whithersoe'r she came, the well-foreseeing Vala: wolves she tamed, magic arts she knew, magic arts practiced; ever was she the joy of evil people.[42]

The first incarnations—Heid and Gullveig—are therefore earlier forms of Angrboða, who is a powerful sorceress, not just a giantess. Rydberg even goes so far as to claim her to be the female

---

[41] RYDBERG, V., *Teutonic Mythology*, 100

[42] THORPE, B., *The Elder Edda of Saemund Sigfusson*, 7

counter-part of Loki, saying that Loki, "through Heid's arrival, found his other-ego and when the evil principle, hitherto barren, could as a man and woman give birth to evil deeds".[43] This suggests that the catalyst is the union of the destructive aspects in both the masculine and feminine psyche. Loki, then, has two wives, the good one who is a God, and the evil one who is a giantess, which draws attention to his role as a half-breed and outsider. Angrboða, though her relationship with Loki, not only brings forth 'evil deeds', but also Hel, Jörmungandr, and Fenrir. However, this is not the end of Angrboða's role, for she is also the same Angrboða who dwells in the Iron Wood, guarding the Sword of Victory until such time as it can be given to the fire-giant in preparation for Ragnarök. Moreover, her time spent in Iron Wood is not idle, for she also raises the offspring of her child Fenrir, as is illustrated by the following passage from the *Völupsá*:

> In the east, she sat, the old one,
> in Iron Wood,
> and bred there
> the broods of Fenrir.
> There will come from them all
> one of that number
> to be a moon snatcher
> in troll's skin. (Dronke 1997:17)[44]

---

[43] RYDBERG, V., *Teutonic Mythology*, 100

[44] GANSUM, T., Role the Bones – From Iron to Steel in *Norwegian Archeological Review*, 37:1 (UK: Routledge, 2004), 46

In relation to this passage, it has been suggested that an analogy can be drawn between the 'broods of Fenrir' and weaponry. It could be a reference to a forge, with birth as a metaphor for the crafting of weapons. The author puts forward a case for this allegory in the extract below,

> The poem *Völuspá* builds up toward Ragnarök in stanza 40, and what could be more appropriate than weapons? To conclude, I believe that it is the birth of iron and steel that takes place in this stanza. The one who devours the sun/moon is the furnace/forge where the smith works. And a shining weapon, used in the final battle, is the one in troll's skin (shining and brilliant i.e. steel). In "*Alvismál*", "*Dvalins leica*" is the name of the sun, but it can also indicate a trap or betrayal [...] Dwarfs function in and through technologies, things, and actions. They were born before the humans, and we know of over 60 dwarf names in *Völuspá*. Dwarfs and horses are connected to the sun. The horses Rimfakse and Skinfakse pull the sun, and under the shoulders, the Æsir-Gods placed wind bellows, hidden powers and iron keels [...] very reminiscent of the activities in the smithy.[45]

This explanation relates to the larger framework of the narrative, for although some of the havoc

---

[45] GANSUM, T., Role the Bones – From Iron to Steel in *Norwegian Archeological Review*, 37:1, pp. 46-7

wrought during Ragnarök can be attributed to environmental issues, many of the tragic events which arise in the prophecy can be attributed to human action and not that of either Gods nor any of Loki's brood; war, greed, and discord are caused by men in the world of Miðgarðr, and it not until the advent of war that the progressive degeneration rapidly accelerates, finally reaching its climax in total annihilation.

> Broken was the outer wall of the sir's burgh. The Vanir, foreseeing conflict, tramp o'er the plains. Oðinn cast [his spear], and mid the people hurled it: that was the first warfare in the world.[46]

Thus, once the spear is cast, war is created in Miðgarðr, and from this point onwards Angrboða is free to generate war from within the Iron Wood. Even the name 'Iron Wood' is suggestive of a place which is unnatural, and where weapons sprout like trees. This war will later increase to catastrophic proportions. This will be preceded, however, by a terrible winter, which continues unbroken by spring for three years. This is the Fimbul-winter.

> In the first place will come the winter, called Fimbul-winter, during which snow will fall from the four corners of the world; the frosts will be very severe, the wind piercing, the weather tempestuous, and the sun impart no

---

[46] THORPE, B., *The Elder Edda of Saemund Sigfusson*, 7

> gladness. Three such winters shall pass without being tempered by a single summer. Three other similar winters follow, during which war and discord will spread over the whole globe. Brethren for the sake of mere gain shall kill each other, and no one shall spare either his parents or his children.[47]

What begins with winter culminates in war; this is when Ragnarök truly begins, and it also when one of the most curious incidents present in the myth occurs: the release of Naglfar, the ship built from the fingernails of the dead.

> Further forward I see, much can I say of Ragnarök and the Gods' conflict. Brothers shall fight, and slay each other; cousins shall kinship violate. The earth resounds, the giantesses flee; no man will another spare. Hard is it in the world, great whoredom, an axe age, a sword age, shields shall be cloven, a wind age, a wolf age, ere the world sinks.[48] [...] Hrym steers from the east, the waters rise, the mundane snake is coiled in jotun-rage. The worm beats the water, and the eagle screams: the pale of beak tears carcasses; Naglfar is released.[49]

---

[47] THORPE, B., *The Elder Edda of Saemund Sigfusson*, 206
[48] Ibid., 8
[49] Ibid.

The imagery of Naglfar is odd and nightmarish for it is built with the nails of dead men, and therefore it represents a warning about hygiene, for "if a man dies with uncut nails, then he increases material for the ship Naglfar greatly, which Gods and men would wish to be slow in being built".[50] There is a reason why nails are used to construct Naglfar. Nails have a hidden esoteric meaning in Indo-European cultures, and were believed to be a highly impure part of the body. For example, the technique for the proper disposal of the fingernails mentioned in Aulus Gellius, *Attic Nights* 10.15:

> The ceremonies placed upon the Flamen Dialis are many, and the forbearances are numerous [...] No one should cut the hair of the Dialis except a free man [...] The cuttings of the nails and hair of the Dialis are buried in the earth under a fruitful tree.[51]

The Flamen Dialis were the high priests of ancient Rome, and according to Georges Dumézil are equivalent to the Brahmin of India, whom also consider the nails to be 'impure'. As an impure part removed from the body, they must be disposed of correctly in order to maintain the purity of the priest's body, for they are an extension of it.

---

[50] LINCOLN, B., Treatment of Hair and Fingernails Among the Indo-Europeans in *History of Religions*, Vol. 16, No. 4 (USA: The University of Chicago Press, 1977), 360

[51] Ibid., 354

Traditions of ritual disposal of the nails are also found amongst the Germans. In Oldenburg hair and nails are wrapped in a cloth and fastened under a tree three days before the new moon, to cure infertility. In Brandenburg, Düsseldorf, and Swabia, hair and nails are placed in a hole bored in a tree or are placed on a branch.[52] Both examples use a tree, which is representative of growth, nature, and fertility. There is a subconscious symbolic motif at work here; the man who buried his hair and perhaps his nails in a place covered with grass, under a fruitful tree, or with a prayer for the growth of the vegetation, felt himself to be participating in the cosmogonic drama, recreating the very world with this simple gesture and reestablishing the order on which life depends.[53] On the other hand, however, improper disposal of the nails represents a transgression of the natural order. The image of Naglfar is based on the premise that the improper disposal of hair and nails is an act which threatens the well-being of the cosmos.[54] If proper disposal serves to *perpetuate* the cosmic order, then improper disposal can *negate* it, and create chaos. This is also seen in the Avestan text where Ahura Mazdā warned that demons (*daēvas*) and monsters (*xrafstras*) would spring from hair and nails that were let to fall to earth without proper ritual. Again, nail-clippings were regarded as being impure if not disposed of correctly. Mary Douglas

---

[52] LINCOLN, B., Treatment of Hair and Fingernails Among the Indo-Europeans in *History of Religions*, Vol. 16, No. 4, 355

[53] Ibid., 361

[54] Ibid.

in her work *Purity and Danger* argues that the body is a powerful model or image which corresponds to a system of boundaries that represents the structure of society itself. The extremities of the body—hair, fingernails, and toenails—represent the limits of society, the points at which it is vulnerable to contact with external peripheral regions, and must therefore be treated with appropriate care. She writes that,[55]

> All margins are dangerous. If they are pulled this way or that the shape of fundamental experience is altered. Any structure of ideas is vulnerable at its margins. We should expect the orifices of the body to symbolize its specifically vulnerable points. Matter issuing from them is marginal stuff of the most obvious kind. Spittle, blood, milk, urine, feces, or tears by simply issuing forth have traversed the boundary of the body. So also have bodily parings, skin, nail, hair clippings, and sweat. The mistake is to treat bodily margins in isolation from all other margins. There is no reason to assume any primacy for the individual's attitude to his own bodily and emotional experience, any more than for his cultural and social experience.[56]

What this means, in the context of the human body, is that by being removed from the body, the nails

---

[55] LINCOLN, B., Treatment of Hair and Fingernails Among the Indo-Europeans in *History of Religions,* Vol. 16, No. 4, 352

[56] Ibid.

become impure—indeed, they are twice as impure for not only are they marginal points of the body, they are also dead—the nail clippings are imbued with the 'power of the impure'. In this regard, Mary Douglas perceives the twin poles of the sacred and profane not as antithetical, but as permeating one another. Likewise, Victor Turner sees society as a dialectic interplay of structure and antistructure, hierarchical organization, and egalitarian aspirations, in line with Nietzsche's notion of "the power of the weak".[57] In relation to Nalfagr, the ship represents the transition from the sacred to the profane, violating social and cosmic law. Perversely, it is the collective impurity of this minor body part that generates the collective impetus required for Nalfagr to set sail.

In another version of *Völupsá*, it is Loki himself that steers Nalfagr. In relation to Loki's role as a trickster, and his involvement in the events leading towards Ragnarök, the image of Loki being at the helm of Nalfagr—the ship of impurity—seems quite appropriate.

> Loki brings up the *hřimthursus* and the retinue of Hel (*Heljar sinnar*).[58]

---

[57] KOEPPING, K. P., Absurdity & Hidden Truth: Cunning Intelligence and Grotesque Body Images as Manifestations of the Trickster in *History of Religions*, vol. 24 no. 3, 199

[58] GRIMM, J., *Teutonic Mythology*, Vol. II, 814

> That ship fares from the east: come will Musspell's people o'er the sea, and Loki steers. The monster's kin goes all with the wolf; with them the brother is of Byleist on their course.[59]

The next character to appear with the myth is the enigmatic Surtr.

> Surtr from the south comes with flickering flame; shines from his sword the Val-gods' sun. The stony hills are dashed together, the giantesses totter; men tread the path of Hel, and heaven is cloven.[60]

Finn Magnusen believes that Surtr is an exalted God of light, under whose rule, as opposed to that of Oðinn, the new and universal empire stands.[61] The connection to Muspelheim also suggests that he is, in fact, a God of light in his own right. Surtr (is derived from the word the *sawrt* (swarthy, browned by heat). Volcanic caves in Iceland are called Surtarhellir.[62] This suggests a connection not only to light, but also to fire. The Æsir do battle with Surtr and his host on a holm called Oskopnir.[63] Simek says that "in Iceland, Surtr was obviously thought of as being a mighty giant who ruled the powers of

---

[59] THORPE, B., *The Elder Edda of Saemund Sigfusson*, 8
[60] Ibid., 8
[61] GRIMM, J., *Teutonic Mythology, Vol. II*, 824
[62] Ibid. 809
[63] Ibid., 810

(volcanic) fire of the Underworld", and he compares Surtr to Eldr, Eimnir, and Brandingi, noting that they all appear to be personifications of fire. Bertha Phillpotts also speculates that Surtr was inspired by Icelandic eruptions, and was a volcano demon.

The next adversary with which the Gods must do battle with is the wolf Fenrir. Of all the monstrous children spawned by Loki, Fenrir is the most dangerous; Jörmungandr is thrown into the depths of the ocean, Hel confined within the earth, but Fenrir is so dangerous that the Gods bind the wolf and keep him with them.

> Fenrir however, proves too strong to be confined, and the wolf breaks free. The Gods, having seen this, made another fetter, half as strong again as the former, which they called Dromi, and prevailed on the wolf to put it on, assuring him that, by breaking this, he would give an undeniable proof of his vigor. [...] [Fenrir] breaks it again [...] the dwarfs are sought to make the fetter called Gleipnir. It was fashioned out of six things; to wit, the noise made by the footfall of a cat; the beards of women; the roots of stones; the sinews of bears; the breath of fish; and the spittle of birds. With this bond, the wolf remains bound 'til Ragnarök.[64]

---

[64] THORPE, B., *The Elder Edda of Saemund Sigfusson*, pp. 181-182

The first distinction to note here is that the components of the final fetter which binds the wolf are non-existent abstractions. Hence, we can assume that a metaphor is at work, and that the true nature of the binding is both esoteric and invisible. Secondly, 'Gleipnir' is a magic fetter, fashioned at Oðinn's instructions to be delicate in appearance, but enormously strong. This point was of particular interest to Georges Dumézil, who understood Oðinn as a master of magic, particularly the power to bind.[65] Dumézil's main hypotheses was a theory of dual sovereignty which he claimed was integral to all Indo-European civilizations, and is described in his seminal work *Mitra-Varuna*. The basic premise of this is that Indo-European mythology outlines the political ideologies of the era, and that dual sovereignty was depicted by deities that ruled as a pair—a one-eyed magician and a one-handed jurist—who defined the two sides of Indo-European sovereignty, with instances found in Roman, Irish, and Indic myths.[66] In the case of the Northern Tradition, they obviously correspond to Oðinn and Tyr. It is Oðinn who orders the binding of Gleipnir, which binds the wolf, and it is Tyr who loses his hand to the jaws of the wolf.

---

[65] LINCOLN, B., Rewriting the German War God: Georges Dumézil, Politics and Scholarship in the Late 1930s in *History of Religions*, Vol. 37, No. 3 (USA: University of Chicago Press, 1998), 196

[66] Ibid., 197

This notion of paired sovereignty was accompanied by a third element in Dumézil's theory, that of a third class or caste, which fitted into a trifunctional model of society. What is of particular interest at this point, is that when writing on this topic, Dumézil deliberately decided to use a shortened version of Snorri's retelling of the myth[67] which omits several important details. As a result of this, Dumézil defined the model incorrectly, writing that the "Scandinavian triad is defined in precisely this way: Oðinn, the sovereign magician; Thôrr, the champion-thunderer; Freyr (or Njödhr), lubricious and peaceful producer."[68] Had he used the longer version instead, it would have been clear that the second function should be allocated to Tyr. Moreover, in the extended rendition, Snorri elaborates further on the Gods treatment of the wolf:

> The Gods raised the wolf and give it food. And when the Gods saw how much he grew each day, and all the prophecies said he might be destined to do them harm, then they adopted a plan.[69]

---

[67] At the time of composition, Dumézil had concerns about the rise of National Socialism in Germany, and for this reason he chose to down play both the role of Tyr as a war God and the nature of the wolf.

[68] DUMEZIL, G., trans. COLTMAN, D., *Mitra-Varuna: An Essay on Two Indo-European Representations of Sovereignty* (USA: Zone Books, 1988), 121

[69] LINCOLN, B., Rewriting the German War God: Georges

It is worth noting here that the wolf is indicated to grow at an accelerated rate, and it is the wolf's increasing size that alarms the Gods and causes them to bind the wolf.

> Finally, the wolf himself loses a bodily member, complementing the losses suffered by Oðinn and Tyr. Then the wolf answered: "It seems to me there's no renown to be had from that ribbon, even if I tear asunder so thin a band. But if it is made with craft, even though it may seem small, that band won't come off my foot."[70]

Of further significance is the fact that it is the wolf which causes Tyr to lose his hand:

> Tyr's hand is placed in the wolf's mouth at *vedhi*, "as surety," so that he will permit himself to be bound. This word (*vedh*, neuter) is the same one that still subsists in the modern German *wette*, "wager," in the Swedish *staa vad*, "to wager," and even in the French *gage, gager*, "pledge, to wager."[71]

Dumézil, Politics and Scholarship in the Late 1930s in *History of Religions*, Vol. 37, No. 3, 197

[70] LINCOLN, B., Rewriting the German War God: Georges Dumézil, Politics and Scholarship in the Late 1930s in *History of Religions*, Vol. 37, No. 3, 198

[71] DUMEZIL, G., trans. COLTMAN, D., *Mitra-Varuna: An Essay on Two Indo-European Representations of Sovereignty*, 122

Thus, a legislation or pledge is placed upon the wolf, the price of which is Tyr's hand. Furthermore, it is this legislation which is the real invisible bond which keeps Fenrir bound, as is implied by the fact that none of the ingredients of Gleipnir are physical objects – the wolf has been bound by law and nothing else, hence the strength and invisibility of the bond.

Dumezil's theory is based on comparative mythology, in which a deity representing the sovereign function is indicated by the loss of an eye, and the loss of a hand indicates the warrior or legislative aspect of a deity. A special meaning is also indicated by the binding or injury to the lower body parts.

> A wound to the head or eye marks those who are sovereign (by virtue of royalty, sacrality, knowledge, magic, and/or righteousness); a wound to the hand or arm, marks those of martial power; and wounds to the lower body mark low-ranking persons, whose appetites for food or wealth may be perceived as ignoble or dangerous, and who are reduced to positions of servile captivity.[72]

What is unfolding then in the story of Fenrir is a parable of a vertical hierarchy in which the loss

---

[72] LINCOLN, B., Rewriting the German War God: Georges Dumézil, Politics and Scholarship in the Late 1930s in *History of Religions*, Vol. 37, No. 3, 200

of an eye gives rise to the top-ranked sovereign function, represented by Oðinn; the loss of a hand, to the intermediate warrior function, represented by Tyr; and the loss of a foot to a lower function, represented by Fenrir.[73]

Several other German narratives describe this same motif, but with slight differences – in place of an eye, one sometimes finds the head or other parts thereof; in place of a hand, the arm; and in place of a foot, the leg or another part of the lower body.[74] Here, the myth emphasizes the lower order's propensity for consumption (rather than production), depicting the wolf's appetite and capacity for growth as the threat the Gods check with their defining powers of trickery, magic, and force.[75] With Freyr representing the third level of the hierarchy, the wolf must, therefore, be assigned a fourth function: the laborer class, who like the wolf, do not produce, but are instead employed by the three higher social functions of sovereigns, warriors/legislators, and farmers/craftsmen. This class is associated with the lack of production or creativity, hence the rapid growth and voracious consumerism. Thus, when unbound the wolf represents social chaos, and mob rule. The invisible fetter which keeps Fenrir bound is the same as the

---

[73] LINCOLN, B., Rewriting the German War God: Georges Dumézil, Politics and Scholarship in the Late 1930s in *History of Religions*, Vol. 37, No. 3, 198

[74] Ibid.

[75] Ibid.

legislation which controls society; it is nothing more than an intangible law. Furthermore, it can be seen as a symbol of the ages themselves, with the wolf being finally released in the appropriately entitled 'Wolf Age'. At the end of the Wolf Age, Fenrir slays the sovereign God Oðinn, which is a metaphor for the reign of evil and chaos.

> Then arises Hlin's second grief, where Oðinn goes with the wolf to flight and bright slayer of Beli with Surtr. Then will Frigg's beloved fall.[76]

Oðinn's death will then be avenged by his son Vidar, who will slay the beast Fenrir.

> Then comes the great victor-sire's son, Vidar, to fight with the deadly beast. He with his hands will make his sword pierce to the heart of the giant's son: then avenges his father.[77]

Fenrir, however, is not the only scion of Loki whom the Gods must engage in combat, they must also battle the Miðgarðr Serpent Jörmungandr. As mentioned previously, Jörmungandr is a metaphor for the rotation of the earth around the sun – thus, unlike the wolf which is indicative of a social disordering, Jörmungandr is a natural disaster. In the next passage, Jörmungandr allies himself with the wolf to vomit poison into the airs and waters.

---

[76] THORPE, B., *The Elder Edda of Saemund Sigfusson*, 8
[77] Ibid., 8

As Jörmungandr is mentioned as placing himself beside the wolf, this seems like a problem which may be man-made: namely pollution or an interference with nature that becomes a threat to all life on earth. Finally, amidst the ensuing death and chaos, Surtr comes, and Jörmungandr is slain.

> The Miðgarðr serpent, placing himself by the side of the wolf, vomits forth floods of poison which overwhelm the air and waters. Amidst this devastation, heaven is cleft in twain, and the sons of Muspell ride through the breach. Surtr rides first, and both before and behind him flames burning fire. His sword outshines the sun itself.[78]

> Then comes the mighty son Hlodyn: (Oðinn's son goes with the monster to fight); Miðgarðr's Veor in his rage will slay the worm. Nine feet will go Fiorgyn's son, bowed by the serpent, who feared, no foe. All men will their homes forsake.[79]

During the conflict, Freyr fights with Surtr, Oðinn fights with Fenrir, Thôrr with Jörmungandr, Heimdall with Loki, and in every case the Gods die, along with Loki and Fenrir.

---

[78] THORPE, B., *The Elder Edda of Saemund Sigfusson*, 297
[79] Ibid., 8

As the symbolism of Surtr has already been discussed there is no need to repeat the material already cited – suffice to say that Surtr is definitely associated with fire, but it is a fire of destructive purification that cleanses the earth of the impurity deployed by Loki. Since it is a global form of destruction, it is highly unlikely that Surtr represents a volcano, especially as he is said to 'ride through' from a breach in the sky. This sounds more akin to a comet crashing into the earth, or another catastrophe of celestial origin. Only an event of this magnitude would have the capability of extinguishing virtually all life on earth.

> The sun darkens, earth in ocean sinks, fall from heaven the bright stars, fire's breath assails the all-nourishing tree, towering fire plays against heaven itself.[80]

Life does not perish entirely, however – Baldr and Höðr, survive the apocalypse, due to their absence. They are, therefore, named in *Völuspâ* (Sæm. 10b), as surviving Gods, since they were not involved in the struggle with Surtr.

> Unsown shall the fields bring forth, all evil be amended; Baldr shall come; Höðr and Baldr, the heavenly Gods, Hropt's glorious dwellings shall inhabit. Understand ye yet, or what?[81]

---

[80] THORPE, B., *The Elder Edda of Saemund Sigfusson*, 8
[81] Ibid., 9

FATE & THE TWILIGHT OF THE GODS

The parents of the future population, hidden deep inside the earth in Mimir's Holt at the bottom of the world tree, also survive to repopulate the earth, preserved not by the physical nourishment which arises from the tree, the axis mundi, but the wisdom which is its nourishment. Once they emerge to safely experience the regenerated earth, the golden tablets are rediscovered, as is the universal law which held sway in the Axe Age.

> Mimir's Holt, Hoddmimir's Holt, the subterranean grove, where the children who are to be the parents of the future race of man have their secure abode until the regeneration of the world, living on the morning-dew which falls from the world-tree, *hrdr vidr*, "the tree rich in sap".[82]

> There again, the wondrous golden tables in the grass are found, which in days of old had possessed the ruler of the Gods and Fiolnir's race.[83]

As for the fate of the Gods,

> In the realm of the Gods it is Viðar and Vali (Sn.76) who revive Asgarð on Iðavöllr, and with them are associated Môði and Magni, beside Baldr and Höðr from the underworld;

---

[82] RYDBERG, V., *Teutonic Mythology*, 67

[83] THORPE, B., *The Elder Edda of Saemund Sigfusson*, 8

> Viðar and Vali are the two avengers, one having avenged Oðinn's death on Fenrisŭlf, the other's Baldr's death on Höðr. They two, and Baldr the pure blameless God of light are sons of Oðinn, while, Môði and Magni appear as sons of Thôrr by a gŷgr, and from that time they bear the emblem of his might, the all-crushing Miölnir. Unquestionably this means, that Oðinn and Thôrr, the arch-gods of old Asgarð, come into sight no more, but are only renewed in their sons.[84]

And,

> After the world conflagration or *Surtalogi*, a new and happier earth rises out of the sea, with Gods made young again, but still called Æsir.[85]

Finally, *Völuspá* ends with an ominous note. Even this new Golden Age shall not be eternal, and Níðhöggr, the force of entropy and dissolution, is dropped onto the earth, where she will again gnaw at the roots of the revitalized world tree until the cycle reaches its conclusion again.

> She a hall standing than the sun brighter, with gold bedecked, in Gimill: there shall be righteous people dwell, and forevermore

---

[84] GRIMM, J., *Teutonic Mythology, Vol. II*, 823
[85] Ibid., 815

happiness enjoy. Then comes the dark dragon flying from beneath, Níðhöggr the glistening serpent, from Nida-fels. On her wings bears, flying o'er the plain, a corpse. Now she will descend.[86]

CONCLUSION

Now that all the components which make up the story of Ragnarök have been examined, they need to be looked at in integration. The first and most important aspect of this is Loki, who is clearly the antagonist behind the events which lead towards Ragnarök. Throughout the Nordic myths, Loki is set up in a dual role as both a trickster and outsider archetype. In the beginning, he is a mostly benign trickster deity, who by virtue of his role as an outsider, is able to transgress boundaries in the service of the other Gods. There is, however, an element of tension in this role, because even though he is a 'blood brother' to Oðinn, Loki is never fully accepted into the community of Asgarð. By virtue of his parentage, he is considered to be an outsider, which is the source of his 'impurity'. His social impurity is continuously emphasized, for which he is eventually imprisoned and tortured until Ragnarök. This is a rather harsh punishment for

---

[86] THORPE, B., *The Elder Edda of Saemund Sigfusson*, 9

Loki, so it is not entirely surprising that he ceases performing as an essentially harmless trickster, and adopts a stance of murderous villainy. Likewise, his binding beneath the earth and his children (Hel and Jörmungandr) add credence to the fact that he is not a fire deity, but rather a chthonic one. In his relations with Oðinn, his intelligence is of a similar level – but the distinction between them is that Oðinn uses his intelligence to *forestall* Ragnarök and Loki uses his to *enact* it; seen in this light he is akin to the mirror image of Oðinn. Loki functions as both blood brother and adversary to Oðinn, and is destined to be cast in the role of the villain because of his impure ancestry arising from giant blood. This also raises the question of predestination or *ørlog* (OS. Ørlog "fate" – fixing from the first), for Oðinn is said to know all and yet "Oðinn and all the âses cannot prevent the misfortune of Baldr […] Ragnarök, the destruction of the world, far over-tops the power of the Gods."[87] This suggests that Ragnarök arises from a mistake made by Oðinn himself, and because he made it, this is the one act Oðinn cannot prevent. His initial acceptance and kindness towards Loki is an event which cannot revoked, and the consequences of allowing Loki to cohabit with the Gods is the catalyst which causes Ragnarök. Oðinn, who never fully accepts Loki or drives him away, is the root cause of Loki's evil and resentment. Loki, is to a certain extent, the shadow function of Oðinn, whom he neither embraces nor rejects. Ragnarök,

---

[87] GRIMM, J., *Teutonic Mythology*, Vol. II, 856

therefore, can only be forestalled and not prevented, because it is an event which arises from a mistake made in Oðinn's past, *and that specific mistake is his treatment of Loki.* This interpretation not only reveals the esoteric issues surrounding Ragnarök, but also encapsulates the full tragedy of the event – that Oðinn made a mistake in extending friendship to Loki, but never fully accepted or denied him as a member of society, and because this initial act of kindness was an error of judgment made by Oðinn himself, he is powerless to prevent the course of actions which lead to Ragnarök, and the doom of the Gods.

As the main antagonist in Ragnarök, the aspects of Loki which were originally benign deteriorate, beginning with the appearance of the three-fold woman from Jötunheimr – in the presence of her giantess and magical nature, the inherent impurity within Loki awakens and his harmless trickster impulses shift towards planned malevolence. In one version of the myth this will culminate in conspiring to murder Baldr, in the other his social transgression – both of which lead to him being bound underground until the advent of Ragnarök, when he will finally break free. Then, Loki will construct Naglfar, the impurity from the liminal margins of society, which disrupts the boundaries of social order, allowing for Loki's allies to arise – the wolf which unleashes the anger of the mob in pure chaos, war and weaponry crafted by Angrboða, and Jörmungandr, the destruction and poisoning of the natural environment. Finally, Surtr unleashes the final cataclysm that purifies the earth of the decay and impurity spawned by Loki.

The structure of the myth holds very little in common with that of the Christian apocalypse, and it is aligned more closely with the Hindu Yugas. A theme of gradual degeneration is present in both cycles, reflecting on the loss of social order and the need for legislation. The main difference lies in the way in which the narrative unfolds. In Hinduism Kalki is embodied as a hero who purges the earth to renew the cycle. Surtr is, by comparison, an obscure figure whom the surviving texts do not fully describe. There are no traces of Christian influence in *Völuspá*, and it has more in common with Hinduism, which suggests that *Völuspá* predates the advent of Christian monotheism.

One thing, however, is very clear: Ragnarök is not a natural disaster, rather its events are born from the actions of humans and Gods – as such, like Oðinn and Loki, humans have both the power to forestall the event or accelerate its destruction.

Made in the USA
San Bernardino, CA
02 April 2019